# THE AEC MANDATOR
## By Graham Edge

## ACKNOWLEDGEMENTS

My thanks as usual go to Neil Mitchell for his customary diligence in searching out appropriate material from the vast archive at the British Commercial Vehicle Museum. Once again he has located some outstanding photographs. Richard Brent contributed a couple of important photos of his father's small fleet. Rufus Carr and Tony Petch have contributed stunning pictures from New Zealand and Australia. Over the years many people have assisted me and I record my grateful appreciation to you all.

### Photographic Credits

Many of the photographs used in this book are official AEC material. Most of the negatives are in the care of the British Commercial Vehicle Museum Trust Archives. Any material reproduced from other sources has been duly accredited in the caption. Every effort has been made to trace all original copyright holders if there was any doubt.

The Commercial Vehicles Archive Series is produced and published by Gingerfold Publications in conjunction with the British Commercial Vehicle Museum Trust Archives.

This title was first published in October 2005 by Gingerfold Publications, 8 Tothill Road, Swaffham Prior, Cambridge, CB5 0JX.
Email: gingerfold@ukonline.co.uk Website: www.gingerfold.com

### Copyright

Graham Edge, Gingerfold Publications, and the British Commercial Vehicle Museum Trust Archives.
**ISBN 1 902356 14 4**

### Other titles in this series
AEC Mandator V8 (out of print)
Leyland Atlantean
The Leyland Comet (out of print)
AEC Mammoth Major Mk.III
The Leyland Beaver
The AEC Mercury
The AEC Mustang and Marshal
The Leyland Octopus

Printed by The Burlington Press, Foxton, Cambridge CB2 6SW

# INTRODUCTION

There is no doubt that model naming policy adapted by AEC could be confusing to anyone not too familiar with the products of Southall. This was especially so in the 1940s and '50s. Most casual observers probably associate the Matador name with AEC's acclaimed medium artillery tractor, which was a military 4x4 machine produced during World War Two and again in the 1950s. Yet 4x2 Matador Mk.II lorries preceded gun tractors and they were also built in the post-war years when there was no requirement for new vehicles by the armed forces. The civilian Matador Mk.III became the Mandator Mk.III and why this happened is explained in Section 1.

Our old friends the Construction and Use Regulations also played a significant part in Mandator evolution and the 1964-5 statutes caused an important development of the Mandator tractive unit to materialise. This was of course the twin-steer Mammoth Minor tractor, its name being revived from a distinctive AEC six-wheeler of the late 1930s. We shall study this important model in Section 5.

For some fifteen years from 1960 until run-down of production at Southall commenced in the mid-seventies, AEC was producing more lorries per annum than ever before. At the vanguard of the firm's successful assault on home and export commercial vehicle markets was the Mandator Mk.V. Later, the market leading Ergomatic tilt-cabbed design consolidated popularity for AEC's heavyweight tractive units. Was there ever a more stylish lorry cab design than that of an Mk.V? Not only did these lorries look the part, but they were also fast, powerful, and possessed excellent brakes. Drivers loved them. Was there a more productive, cost effective, and profitable articulated lorry than a tilt-cabbed Mandator in the '60s and '70s? Probably not.

It is hard to believe that forty years has passed since the introduction of Ergomatic AECs, and following trail-blazing Mk.V types, these tilt-cabbed Mandators quickly became hugely popular. Purchasers of such AECs comprised a veritable 'who's-who' of British transport companies and own-account fleets. It was a great pity that Mandator development stagnated in a period of rapid advances and when production ended in 1977 the model had become somewhat dated.

Locally in the Bolton area, Hipwood and Grundy of Farnworth, and BRS ran Mandator Mk.Vs in my formative years, and then Ergomatic tilt-cabbed versions soon appeared in quantity in both fleets. HKR Transport of Little Lever had some very early tilt-cabbed Mandators, and drivers soon referred to them as "Man Eaters". In 1966 a custodian of a new AEC Mandator with its 33-foot trailer was envied as being an elite and favoured driver.

As usual with a subject in the "Commercial Vehicles Archive Series" we shall look at the development and service history of the AEC Mandator range from start to finish, supported by a comprehensive photographic selection of these lorries in service.

Graham Edge,
Swaffham Prior, July 2005.

# SECTION 1

## In The Beginning Was The Mandator A Matador?

It is necessary to return to the 1930s to trace the evolution of AEC's Mandator range. Firstly, some understanding of the company's sales policy and its commercial vehicles catalogue must be considered. Undeniably, in the early thirties AEC was primarily a premium quality passenger chassis builder that also manufactured lorries that were built to high standards when time and production capacity permitted. By no means was lorry development neglected, because like all major competing manufacturers, AEC had modernised its designs following the stringent requirements dictated by the 1933 Road and Rail Traffic Act, including Construction and Use Regulations. Because AEC was "builder of London's buses" the very considerable needs of the capital city's bus fleet came first. Not only was AEC supplying the majority of chassis purchased annually by London Transport, it also had considerable business with other city and municipal public transport undertakings. This was similar in some respects to its erstwhile competitor, Leyland Motors, which had equal prominence in passenger chassis markets. But by virtue of being a bigger company with more manufacturing facilities Leyland was also able to produce larger quantities of goods vehicles.

With bus production taking precedence at Southall, AEC tended to specialise its lorry production for the heavyweight market. In the early thirties, Mammoth four-wheelers and Mammoth Major six-wheelers were its main models. AEC gained the distinction of building the first internal combustion engined eight-wheeler lorry in 1934, and thereafter multi-axle six and eight-wheeler Mammoth Majors became the mainstays of the company's lorry business. To complete the revised, post-1934 sales catalogue, four-wheeler Monarchs were available and a lighter model, namely the Mercury was also listed. The Mammoth name was retained for mainly export market models and all lorries were available with a choice of petrol or oil (diesel) engines. Four-cylinder oil engines generally powered Monarchs and Mercurys if diesel fuel was the preference of the purchaser. There was a comprehensive availability of different types when it is realised that four-wheelers could be either normal or forward control designs.

From its earliest days AEC was an engineering led concern that always maintained close relationships with customers. Frequent joint discussions between senior AEC engineers and their counterparts at London Transport amply illustrated this. Together, AEC and London Transport agreed all new bus chassis developments for London, considered to be the most demanding bus operating urban conurbation in the world. This policy of regular feedback from operators extended to other AEC buyers large and small. As a consequence of input from AEC users, Southall was always willing to modify lorries to the particular needs of operators.

The original AEC Mandator lorry, chassis type 669, first appeared in 1931 to fulfil the special requirements of certain hauliers that wanted low height chassis vehicles for carrying machinery, or for bodying as furniture vans. These forward control four-wheelers were similar to passenger chassis and in 1932 a normal control, bonneted version appeared. This was type 672, but production of this model was discontinued in the following year because very few, if any at all, had been assembled. Type 669 chassis were augmented in 1932 by model 645, and both Mandator designs were available until 1935. A bonneted version, type 646 reappeared in 1934, but was discontinued the following year. Thereafter if a low chassis lorry was ordered a modified Regal single deck bus chassis was normally supplied. Several Regals served as furniture vans and Pilkington Brothers, the St. Helens based glass manufacturer ran a noted fleet of flat platform bodied Regal Mk.IIIs until the late 1960s.

In the 1930s the vast majority of drawbar trailer prime movers were four-wheelers. This was dictated by the legal requirement for the lorry to be no longer than 26 feet overall, thus eliminating most conventional six-wheelers, although twin-steering 'Chinese-Sixes' could be seen pulling trailers. Eight-wheelers were disqualified on length and also because there was no payload advantage in towing a trailer with such a lorry. The 1933 legislation decreed that the maximum gross vehicle, or train weight, was 22 tons on more than three axles. Hence, an identical rating for both a solo rigid eight and a four-wheeler and trailer. It was not until 1942 and the wartime necessities of maximising road transport resources that the length and weight laws were relaxed and eight-wheelers were allowed to pull drawbar trailers.

To meet the demands for a four-wheeler suitable for drawbar trailer duties, AEC was forced to build a lorry with more power than its four-cylinder engined Monarch. Leyland Motors had an extensive range of lorries including various Beaver models with six-cylinder engines. (See "Commercial Vehicles Archive Series" title, *The Leyland Beaver*). To compete in that market AEC introduced a more powerful prime mover with a choice of either six-cylinder petrol or diesel engines. If the lorry were intended for solo work only, the Monarch name was retained. If it were destined for trailer duties then a new model name, Matador, was adapted. It was slightly confusing in that whether six-cylinder Monarch or Matador, the same chassis type designation was used. This was 346 for petrol versions, or O346 if diesel powered. Matador articulated tractor units for semi-trailers also became available, but in the 1930s heavyweight articulated lorries were not very numerous and Scammell was prominent in that particular category. It can be deduced that AEC was probably the first commercial vehicles builder to design a dedicated model specifically for drawbar trailer work.

The Matador Mk.II, type O346 diesel or 346 petrol, was introduced in 1936 with a solo rating of 12 tons gross weight and 22 tons train weight with a drawbar trailer. This also applied to Matador tractive units with appropriate trailers. Officially there was no Mk.I version, but dates on archive photos suggest that the Matador name was used before the introduction of Mk.IIs. AEC used Mk.II, Mk.III etc. series nomenclature from the mid-1930s until 1965 for concurrent passenger and goods vehicles designs. The first Matador Mk.IIs were forward control lorries and three wheelbases were listed for load carrying duties. These were 12 feet 1 inch for tipper work, 14 feet 7 inches, and 16 feet 7 inches. Normal control, bonneted versions, were introduced a few months later for overseas customers. That chassis range was designated O246 or 246, and a few British customers purchased some despite most domestic operators strongly favouring forward control lorries in the mid-1930s.

By the time Matador Mk.IIs were entering service AEC had developed its diesel engines sufficiently for them to be standard reliable fitments in lorries. Alternatively, customers who were yet to be convinced of the merits of diesel propulsion could specify petrol units.

AEC's first commercially successful oil (diesel) engine was an 8.8 litre unit with indirect fuel injection AEC-Ricardo combustion chambers, and CAV-Bosch injection pump. With a bore and stroke of 115mm x 142 mm it produced 130 bhp at 2,400 rpm, which was relatively high for that time. Then, as the A165 engine it was de-rated slightly for improved reliability and produced 120 bhp. During the first few years of the thirties AEC developed other diesel engines including the two overhead camshaft four-cylinder units used in Monarchs, Mercurys, and some passenger chassis. There was also a 6.6 litre six-cylinder unit wet liner design. One common feature of all these engines was indirect fuel injection, using pre-combustion chamber cylinder heads developed jointly by AEC and the Ricardo Engineering Consultancy. There were three versions known as Ricardo-Comet Mark 1, Mark 2, and Mark 3. AEC persisted with indirect fuel injection engines for longer than its main competitors, Leyland Motors, and other chassis builders that fitted proprietary Gardner diesel engines. L. Gardner and Sons Limited pioneered direct injection small diesel engines with firstly its L2 range in 1929, and its lighter automotive LW series in 1931. By 1933 Leyland had switched to direct injection, but it was not until early in 1936 that AEC offered its customers the choice of either direct or indirect fuel injection. Benefits provided by direct injection were better fuel economy, smoother running, and much easier cold starting. It is understood that the main reason AEC retained its policy of indirect injection was because of its close working relationship with London Transport. That organisation believed that indirect injection diesel engines were quieter and therefore less intrusive to passengers that had grown accustomed to almost silent petrol units.

By the year 1936 AEC had designed yet another six-cylinder diesel engine. This was destined to become one of the renowned commercial vehicle and industrial engines of the twentieth century. Although known as the 7.7 litre, its swept volume was in fact 7.581 litres by virtue of its stroke of 105mm and bore of 146mm. Incidentally, AEC was unusual amongst contemporary British engine manufacturers in quoting cylinder dimensions metrically. Almost every other major engine manufacturer used imperial measurements. Early 7.7 litre engines were once again indirect injection units (A171) with Ricardo-Comet Mark 1 combustion chambers. Power output was 115 bhp at 2,000 rpm, with 325 lbs. ft. of torque at 1,200 rpm. Early Matador Mk.II lorries were fitted with 7.7 litre A171 engines. It is also quite conceivable that 8.8 litre units could have been used in some Matadors, as versions of this engine remained in limited production until the outbreak of the Second World War. However, by 1937 a direct injection 7.7 litre had become the standard engine and as type A173 it produced 95 bhp at 1,800 rpm and 310 lbs. ft. of torque at 1,100 rpm.

Even in 1936, and until 1939, there were still lorry customers with preferences for petrol engines, and AEC would fit its own six-cylinder spark ignition unit into a Matador Mk.II if specified by an operator. An AEC petrol engine was some 7 hundredweights lighter than a diesel, but the potential gain in payload was insufficient to recoup additional fuel costs. AEC's big petrol engine was of 7.04 litres capacity with a bore and stroke of 110 mm by 130 mm. With a single Solex MV46 carburettor this unit had an RAC rating of 45 horsepower and normally produced 120 bhp at a governed speed of 2,400 rpm. A useful amount of torque, 328 lbs. ft. at 1,300 rpm, was transmitted. Magneto ignition was standard, or alternatively, a high-tension coil ignition could be fitted.

Whichever engine powered a Matador Mk.II a 'silent third' four-speed constant mesh gearbox was in unit construction with it. A clutch with 16 inches diameter friction plate was fitted. A two-speed auxiliary gearbox was optional to cope with the demands of trailer work, and this was often known as a "Dual-High" gearbox. In effect it was arranged so that high ratio could only be engaged with fourth speed in the main gearbox to provide a direct drive ratio of 1:1. Fourth gear with low ratio in the auxiliary unit provided a ratio of 1:58:1. The transmission was completed by a double reduction rear axle with standard ratio of 8.1:1 if a lower revving diesel engine was fitted, or 9.3:1 if the faster petrol unit was used. Either ratio could be specified as an alternative, along with a very low gearing of 10.6:1. The standard back axle ratios gave a top speed of 35 mph with 36 x 8 tyres, although lorries and drawbar trailers were legally limited to 16 mph top speed in 1936.

Incidentally, one attraction offered by newly introduced rigid eight-wheelers in 1934 was their slightly higher top speed of 20 mph. There also was no need for the presence of a second man, or driver's mate, in the cab as was required by law with a lorry and trailer. Therefore wages costs were lower for a rigid eight, and such an AEC Mammoth Major Mk.II could legally carry up to 15 tons payload within the 22 tons gross weight limit. In comparison, a Matador Mk.II and trailer was heavier unladen allowing a payload of 14 to 14.5 tons, so with an eight-wheeler option being more profitable for an operator this type quickly became popular. By the end of the 1930s the legal top speed limit anomaly of 4 mph had been eradicated and all heavy lorries were restricted to 20 mph until 1957.

A driver's mate, second man, or trailer boy, (to use all the common descriptions), was essential in the 1930s to operate the trailer brakes of a lorry and trailer outfit. To use another term familiar to those in the transport industry would be "wagon and drag". The mate had a large Neate's hand lever to assist the lorry's braking system by activating those of the trailer when needed. Matador Mk.II lorries generally had vacuum assisted hydraulic braking systems, although triple servo vacuum actuation could also be specified. A multiple pull, ratchet handbrake was used for parking. In later years lorry and trailer brakes were designed to be part of the same system causing the duties of the mate to become redundant although his presence was required in the cab until the late 1960s

Sales of Matador Mk.IIs were steady rather than spectacular for the four years they were in production until the outbreak of World War Two in September 1939 curtailed production. Whilst these were fine, reliable lorries, they were not as numerous as Leyland Beavers for drawbar trailer duties. With war looming AEC was developing a famous model which would "borrow" the Matador model name for a few years. This was of course the legendary 4x4 medium artillery tractor for the War Office, and as a Matador O853 it could have not been given a more appropriate name. With AEC at Southall concentrating its considerable engineering and manufacturing resources on military requirements from late 1939, production of goods and passenger chassis for civilian customers almost ceased. Some Mammoth Majors and Mammoth Minors were assembled for allocation to selected operators under the auspices of the Ministry of Supply and Ministry of War Transport. Interestingly, a few Matador Mk.II lorries were converted to twin-steering 'Chinese-Six' configuration by AEC's regional service depots to provide additional carrying capacity.

*Pilkington Brothers of St. Helens ordered three type 669 Mandators in 1932/33. These were very similar chassis to type 645. The low height is apparent from this historic photo, taken outside Oswald Tillotson's depot. These lorries had under slung rear springs. Pilkington later used Regal single deck coach chassis for carrying large sheets of plate glass, and bought forty-five conventional Mandators between 1960-70. (Negative 1803)*

*In total only 19 Mandators were built in the 1930s, 13 forward control chassis and 6 bonneted lorries. This low height van worked for Crompton Parkinson, manufacturers of electrical equipment. (Negative 5590)*

*A very early Matador that might even pre-date the official introduction of the Mk.II range if the date on the negative (September 1933) is accurate. It was loaded with cement in hessian sacks for delivery to a construction site. (Negative 1400)*

*An interesting view of how a Matador was loaded from an overhead railway. The cab was very basic with no side windows and it is possible that this lorry did not even have tipping gear, meaning its load would have to shovelled off manually. (Negative 1618)*

*The location was almost certainly Trafford Park for the shot of this Matador which was registered in Salford and worked in the fleet of CWS Glass Works at Pendleton. It hauled glass bottles and jars to associate factories of the CWS. (Negative 1438)*

*Timothys, later Timothy, Whites and Taylor were a chain of high street chemists and household stores that eventually merged with Boots. Timothy's operated several Matadors and trailers. This side opening van was unusual, with a bottom-hinged flap to make a platform. Surely that man wasn't going to attempt to carry the packing case in that fashion? (Negative 2505)*

*An amazing lorry, a bonneted Matador artic. Just look at the steering wheel, the driver would have to look through its spokes. I bet the cab designer was a popular man. The lorry was one of the heavier types in the LMS Railways fleet. (Negative 0039)*

*One of Bowaters' famous AECs with its trailer. Bowaters specialised in newsprint; this one advertising the fact that its next load would be for the "Daily Herald". The 'H' style brackets on the side raves were peculiar to that firm and used for securing the paper reels. (Negative 0040)*

*In its prime the CWS was a massive organisation and ran hundreds of lorries. This Matador tanker was used for carrying milk from collection depots in rural districts to urban-based bottling dairies. (Negative 5907)*

*A rare lorry in the London Brick Company fleet. A bonneted Matador with four-in-line trailer. The position of the steering wheel would still encourage a 'sit-up-and-beg driving style, and it must have been difficult for a driver to get leverage on the wheel when manoeuvring. (Negative 5819)*

*A neat Matador gully emptier used by the building department of London Transport. The capital city's transport systems needed a massive support service and were self-sufficient for nearly all its needs. (Negative 5858)*

*Specialist machinery haulier Cliffords of Brentford had a fleet of AECs for its heavy work. A Matador tractor unit with a sturdy low loader semi-trailer. Note the rather puny winch and lack of rear mudguards on the Matador. (Negative 5911)*

*A very early design of ready mixed concrete lorry about to enter service with the grandly entitled Scientific Control Concrete Ltd. These drums were known as agitators and the equipment was mounted on a flat platform rather than bolted directly onto the chassis of the Matador, as became standard practice later. (Negative 0041)*

*Although of indifferent quality, this historically important photograph has been included because it shows one of the AEC Matador Mk.IIs converted to 6x2 'Chinese-Six' configuration during 1941. It is recorded that the lorry was new in 1935 and when rebuilt it had already covered over 300,000 miles. A new 'oil' engine was also fitted. (Photo: Author's collection)*

# SECTION 2

## Why The Matador Mk.III Became The Mandator Mk.III

By 1945 an Allied Forces victory was anticipated. All outstanding orders for the War Office, including 4x4 Matador O853 vehicles, were nearing completion by AEC at Southall. The company's immediate post-war vehicles policy and developments are covered in *AEC Mammoth Major Mk.III*. It will be recalled that AEC offered its basic pre-war Mk.II range, with some modernisation as an interim measure, until Mk.III models were finalised. Like all industrial manufacturing and engineering firms, AEC experienced serious raw materials shortages and rationing of supplies for several years. The necessity of meeting government export targets curtailed chassis availability for home market customers, who were keen to order new vehicles to replace older ones that had worked non-stop during wartime.

Between late 1945 and 1947 multi-axle "interim" AEC Mammoth Majors were an amalgam of pre-war Mk.II components and some features that would be used for a modernised Mk.III range. In contrast the heavyweight AEC four-wheeler for either drawbar or articulated trailer duties was virtually identical in specification to the earlier Matador Mk.II, type O346. Even the post-war Monarch, (type O346S), was standardised with a 7.7 litre engine, and four-cylinder diesel engines were no longer available for road going applications. The six-cylinder petrol engine was also deleted from the sales catalogue.

In the year 1945 there was misplaced optimism in some quarters that the world would be peaceful for some years hence and consequently proven military vehicles, such as 4x4 Matador O853s would not be needed. So, the Matador model name reverted to the 4x2 civilian market drawbar and articulated lorry prime mover, which was given chassis type O347. Its driveline was much as before; 7.7 litre engine, four-speed gearbox supplemented with a two-speed auxiliary unit as an optional extra, and double reduction back axle. One slight difference was that the A173 7.7 litre engine had been uprated to an output of 105 bhp at 1,800 rpm, with 335 lbs. ft. of torque at 1,100 rpm.

There had been no changes in legal gross weights with both Monarchs and Matadors still being for 12 tons as solo lorries, and the Matador remained legally rated for 22 tons gross train weight. In *AEC Mammoth Major Mk.III* the development of another renowned AEC engine, the 9.6 litre, is described and it would be most surprising if A206 versions of this unit were not fitted into a few Matador O347s on the insistence of certain customers. At that stage of its evolution the 9.6 litre engine produced 120 bhp at 1,800 rpm, and 410 lbs. ft. of torque at 1,000 rpm, for lorry applications. (See Appendix B).

By autumn 1947 AEC was able to announce its updated Mk.III range of commercial vehicles. Availability was scheduled for early 1948. These AECs represented a natural progression of development from pre-war Mk.IIs, with new drivelines and braking systems. Unladen weights were heavier and John Rackham, AEC's distinguished and long serving Chief Engineer, was responsible for much of the design of Mk.IIIs.

The AEC Matador Mk.III was a heavy-duty four-wheeler for use as a tipper, solo rigid load carrier or drawbar prime mover, and specialised articulated tractive unit. Gross vehicle weights were as noted earlier in this section. Chassis designation was 3471 for forward control models, and 2481/2/3 for normal control, bonneted lorries destined for overseas clients. (See Appendix A). Generally all home market vehicles were forward control versions 7 feet 6 inches wide, and those for export could be of either layout, left or right hand driving control, and 8 feet 0 inches wide. Four wheelbases were offered; 9 feet 6 inches for the tractive unit, 12 feet 1 inch, 14 feet 7 inches, or 16 feet 7 inches for various load carrying duties such as tipper, tanker, or flat platform. The longest wheelbase Matador Mk.III as a flat platform lorry tared off at approximately 4.25 tons, allowing a legal payload of only 7.75 tons. However, this was some three quarters of a ton lighter than a rival Leyland Beaver 12.B. (See *The Leyland Beaver)*. In those days most haulage contractors would have put at least 10 tons on a Matador Mk.III. With a drawbar trailer the total legal load was about 14.75 tons, and this was very similar to the payload of an articulated version of the model with tandem axle trailer.

Power for a Matador Mk.III came from the 9.6 litre direct injection diesel engine in A216 mode. With a bore of 120 mm and stroke of 142 mm this unit now produced 125 bhp at 1,800 rpm, with 430 lbs. ft. of torque at 1,000 rpm. Either a CAV or Simms fuel injection pump was fitted, with 4-hole injectors. A single, dry friction plate clutch of 15¾ inches diameter with mechanical actuation was used. There was also a clutch brake to permit fast, clean gear changing with the unit mounted five-speed constant mesh, direct drive top, gearbox. This had provision for fitting, if needed, a full power take off running at 600 rpm.

By now there was no optional two-speed auxiliary gearbox, with the driveline being completed by a double reduction, spiral bevel and double helical, rear axle with fully floating half shafts. Standard ratio was 7.0:1 which gave a top speed of 30 mph on 10.00 x 20 tyres. There was a higher alternative of 6.25:1 for a maximum speed of 34 mph, and if specified by a customer, smaller 36" x 8" tyres could be fitted.

The braking system for Matador Mk.IIIs comprised triple vacuum servos on all wheels. Front brakes had individual servo motors with rear brakes being activated by mechanical linkages from the main servo motor. Brake shoes were cam operated and scissors type screw and nut adjusters were used. Drums were 16¾ inches diameter and housed 3 inches wide shoes on the front, with those at the rear being 6 inches wide. The total braking area was 470 square inches. The handbrake operated on the rear wheels only for parking purposes and was a progressive ratchet, mechanical design. All Matadors intended for drawbar trailer work had a Neate's trailer brake and there was also a vacuum pipe coupling for the trailer brakes.

Usually, full air pressure braking was fitted to export models and the compressor was driven from the back of the gearbox off the lay shaft. Home market customers could also specify this braking system.

These lorries had chassis frames fractionally less than 10 inches deep, by 3 inches wide and the steel was ¼ inch thick. AEC worm and nut steering boxes were fitted and the suspension consisted of semi-elliptic springs with rubber bumper pads front and rear. Most chassis had 40 gallons capacity fuel tanks, although tractive units generally carried slightly smaller tanks holding 36 gallons. Electrical components and systems were by either Simms or CAV and were 24 volts. All Matador Mk.IIIs, except tractor units, were equipped with AEC helical spring type towing gear jaws and pin. Cabs were constructed by numerous coachbuilders and completed chassis left Southall with only a front scuttle in place. This surrounded a traditional, exposed Still tube radiator.

By late 1949, because of the "Cold War" between the U.S.S.R. and N.A.T.O., it became apparent to politicians that hope for worldwide peace and stability was unfounded. Re-arming took place and the War Office approached AEC to discuss re-starting assembly of 4x4 Matador O853 artillery tractors. This prompted a model name change for 4x2 Matador Mk.III lorries, the range becoming Mandator Mk.IIIs with chassis designation 3472/4/5 depending upon specification. From then until production of the type ceased almost thirty years later the Mandator name was retained. Somewhat confusingly, exported Mandator Mk.IIIs were still badged as Matador Mk.IIIs until 1957. Normal control versions became type 2472.

In 1954 the Mandator Mk.III range was modified in readiness for higher gross vehicle weights the following year. New maximum weight ratings were 14 tons for the solo lorry and up to 24 tons on four axles for trailer work, whether an articulated lorry or with a drawbar. For overseas customers AEC would agree to a maximum train weight of 36 tons. Since the year 1951 a larger version of the 9.6 litre engine had been available for export markets, and this was the AEC 11.3 litre unit. It now became the standard engine for domestic operators, with the 9.6 being an optional choice. As type A221, the 11.3 litre unit produced 150 bhp at 1,800 rpm, with 505 lbs. ft. of torque at 1,100 rpm. (See *AEC Mammoth Major Mk.III* and Appendix B). This engine retained the same piston stroke dimension of 142 mm as the 9.6 litre engine, but had an increased bore of 130 mm. It also had larger inlet valves.

In effect, these post-1954 Mandator Mk.IIIs were virtually new models. Revised chassis characterisations were introduced; 3481/2/3/4 with the final numerical listing determined by customers' options. Not only did these Mandators have bigger, more powerful engines, they also had stronger and deeper chassis frames of 12 inches by 3 inches made from slightly thicker steel. They were also wider at 8 feet 0 inches and had modernised drivers' structures assembled by various coachbuilders from plans supplied by Southall. Radiators, which were now tube and gill plate blocks, were enclosed behind front grille panels and these modernised cabs became known as "Tin-Fronts".

The five-speed constant mesh gearbox was retained as standard, but a new six-speed overdrive version of the same basic unit became available to order. Revised back axle ratios of 7.12:1 (standard), 6.22:1, and 7.92:1 were listed. The slowest ratio could not be specified with an 11.3 litre engine. Although the long standing 20 mph heavy lorry speed limit was not rescinded until 1957, Mandator Mk.IIIs with overdrive gearboxes were capable of travelling at 40 mph; if the fastest back axle ratio were fitted, then 45 mph was possible.

A completely new braking system that utilised full air pressure was used for these improved Mandator Mk.IIIs. The compressor was still driven from the gearbox if the lorry was intended for solo duties, and it had a single cylinder. If trailer work was envisaged then a twin cylinder compressor was fitted, which was sited remotely from the gearbox and driven by a short propeller shaft. The braking actuation valve was designed so that braking effort was proportional to the foot pressure applied by the driver. Brake shoes were larger at 3½ inches wide on the front wheels, and 6½ inches wide at the rear. Drums were now 15½ inches diameter and the total braking area was 602 square inches. To enable air-braked Mandator Mk.IIIs to handle older, vacuum braked trailers of either type, an exhauster was also fitted with appropriate vacuum breakaway valves incorporated into the braking system. To supplement the lorry's foundation brakes, an exhaust brake was available as an optional extra.

Other available options included hydraulic power assisted steering and a heavy duty back axle. This latter feature was mainly fitted if a Mandator tractive unit was destined for low-loader, abnormal loads work, and if it was an export order for higher train weights. Chassis destined for overseas clients also usually had Marles cam and roller steering boxes.

By the mid-1950s heavyweight tractive units were gradually gaining popularity with hauliers. AEC Mandator Mk.IIIs offered more power and better specifications than most competing makes if gearbox and power steering options were fitted. Leyland Beaver 14.B tractors had similar engine power. (See *The Leyland Beaver*). In particular, BRS favoured Mandator tractive units and as the 1950s progressed these rugged AECs became increasingly familiar sights, not only in the famous Ayres Red livery of the nationalised haulier, but also in colours of other well known firms. Like all AECs of that era Mandators were expected to have lengthy operating lives. Plenty of Mk.IIIs survived into the late 1960s and the introduction of Annual Testing & Plating. Air-braked models would meet interim braking standards for service and secondary brakes with an air-braked trailer. Vacuum braked lorries and trailers could not easily meet new requirements and tended to be scrapped. When final braking standards became applicable in 1972 any remaining Mandator Mk.IIIs were retired. By then they were regarded as obsolete in a rapidly changing period of road transport.

*Matador Mk.IIIs were exported to Australia in reasonable numbers. Often, specifications and wheelbases were peculiar to the importing agent and purchaser. This Australian tractor unit had a much longer wheelbase than the British standard, and it was collecting a couple of tracked machines at one of the Sydney wharves. Note the spelling of Sidney (sic) on the packing cases. (Photo: Douglass Baglin)*

*Another Australian "special" Matador Mk.III artic. with long wheelbase and sleeper cab extension. It was apparently owned by J. Spilvant of Valcluse and was carrying a good load of wool in this picture. Note the absence of any mudguards on the rear wheels and two spare wheel carriers on the trailer.*
*(Photo: Douglass Baglin)*

*A Matador Mk.III engaged on trunking duties between London and West Yorkshire for Harrisons of Dewsbury. With high capacity 'Luton' style van body, and drawbar trailer, its load would have consisted of parcels and small consignments. The roof of the lorry's body was open and covered by a tarpaulin. This enabled it to be loaded and unloaded by overhead hoists at multi-storey mills and warehouses commonplace in its home district. (Photo: Arthur Ingram)*

*A rugged and difficult workplace for a Matador Mk.III in the quarry at Penmeaewar. The lorry is dwarfed by the Ruston Bucyrus excavator, which was dropping some hefty rocks into the special hopper trailer, no doubt destined for the crusher. (Negative 7747)*

*Somewhere in Birmingham in 1955 and a 22-RB excavator on board Lovatt's Mandator Mk.III. The load weight was 22 tons. Points of interest are the ridiculously small driver's mirror, the missing offside headlamp, the different sized spare wheels – one for the trailer and one for the lorry, the red lamps for marking the vehicle if it were left at the roadside overnight, and finally the rather unusual flat fronted cab style. Make's you think doesn't it? (Negative 11445)*

*"You're coming round nicely," maybe that is what the mate was saying to the driver as he reversed this drawbar trailer hauling Mandator Mk.III. It was owned by a subsidiary of George Cohen's 600 Group, well-known scrap and recycling merchants. This company seemed to specialise in lighter materials such as aluminium and tin cans. (Negative 11649)*

*Fleet number 100 in Smith & Robinson's fleet was this Mandator Mk.III artic on contract to Thomas Hedley (later Proctor & Gamble) of Newcastle upon Tyne. It was deployed for hauling phosphates, used in the manufacture of washing powder and detergents. (Negative 11174)*

*A nice side view of a heavy load of round timber on Thames' Mandator Mk.III and Dyson tandem axle trailer. The structure in the background is part of a gasholder. The bolsters appear rather flimsy for that weight and the load could have done with some more chains. Also the load was perilously close to the back of the cab. (Negative 12029)*

Civil engineering contractors Sindall of Cambridge operated this Bonallack cabbed Mandator Mk.III. These cabs were normally used for export vehicles and the top half of the structure could be separated from the bottom half to save height on board ship. The machinery was an early road planer for removing worn out road surfaces. (Negative 0042)

A tin-front cabbed Mandator Mk.III rigid in service in 1958 with LEP. Look at the mixed destination load of packing cases it was carrying and how they were craned on and off the lorry. Those chain grabs relied solely on spikes on the grabs then the converging forces of the chains to hold the cases. You did not want to be standing under one of those. (Negative 16846)

*A typical Australian inter-state outfit of the late 1950s, (ISD 330) based on a 'Tin-Front' Matador Mk.III tractive unit. Again it had a lengthened wheelbase and the cab, with a sleeper "shelf" extension, was constructed by Hastings Deering, the Australian AEC importer. (Photo: Len Bartlett from Tony Petch)*

*The overall legal length permitted in the 1950s was restrictive, so for low weight products high capacity vans were essential to maximise the 24 tons gross weight limit. Because of this four-in-line van trailers could be unstable when loaded on roundabouts and bends unless great care was taken. This nice Mandator Mk.III dates from 1959. (Negative 18342)*

The West Yorkshire woollen towns around Dewsbury specialised in processing waste into products such as felt and fillings for pillowcases. This 1958 Mandator Mk.III rigid was kitted out in typical style for hauling bulky bales, with its platform above the cab and tensioning ratchets. It was also running on very early Michelin X tyres. (Negative 17075)

Westfield of Mansfield were machinery hauliers and their ballast box Mandator was photographed in 1958 at a quarry in Devon during its first trip. It had delivered a new, bigger, excavator and had just loaded the old 19-RB for taking back to Ruston Bucyrus at Lincoln. This lorry survives today restored to all its glory. (Negative 16553)

# SECTION 3

## The Mandator Mk.V Range

Officially, there was no AEC Mk.IV heavyweight goods vehicles range. There were Mk.IV Regal passenger chassis, and as we learned in Section 2, such were the specification differences between early and mid-1950s Mandator Mk.IIIs that conceivably those later lorries could have justified a Mk.IV description.

By the late 1950s articulated lorries were becoming more popular and the majority of Mandator Mk.IIIs ordered were fifth wheel tractive units. With greater flexibility and cheaper initial purchasing costs than, for example, a Mammoth Major eight-wheeler, a Mandator was becoming a preferable alternative for many operators. Eight-wheelers were still numerous in those years, but within a few years things were to change significantly. Road transport was about to enter a transitory period with, amongst other things, the opening of the first Motorways. When older, fully laden lorries were subjected to continuous flat out running for several miles, any weaknesses soon showed and manufacturers had to modify designs for a forthcoming more demanding era of transport. The potential for faster journey times could only be realised with improved engines, overdrive gearboxes, lower ratio back axles, and better braking systems.

At the International Commercial Vehicle Exhibition held at Earls Court in autumn 1958, AEC proudly exhibited its brand new Mk.V range of heavy lorries and passenger vehicles. These were scheduled for production in 1959 and incorporated many features that made them suitable for the dawning Motorway age. The existing Mk.III types were not discontinued immediately and could still be ordered until 1960.

Entirely new chassis designations were introduced for Mk.V vehicles and the Mandator was type G4RA. This was a simplified method; G stood for goods chassis, 4 referred to the number of wheels, R signified right hand control, (with L used for left hand control), and A was a series code. Interestingly, the exhibit Mandator Mk.V unit was placed on the Maudslay stand. In addition to the tractor unit, tipper and load carrier chassis were available. All solo models were for 14 tons gross weight, and for the home market, the gross train weight for articulated or drawbar trailer duties was still restricted to 24 tons, whereas up to 36 tons train weight was permissible in some overseas countries. There was no normal control Mandator Mk.V listed, but a specialised bonneted model with Mandator Mk.V driveline known as a Mogul, type GB4, was introduced at the same time for export customers.

Wheelbases were 8 feet 0 inches for the tractor, 12 feet 5 inches for a tipper or tanker, and a general-purpose rigid length of 15 feet 2 inches for carrying a flat platform body. Later, there was also a longer tractive unit wheelbase of 10 feet 1 inch which became available to special order. As a solo machine a long wheelbase Mandator could legally carry approximately 8 tons, but with a drawbar trailer, or as an articulated lorry with a 26-foot tandem or 4-in-line semi-trailer up to 16 tons payload was possible.

A totally new series of engines was developed for Mk.V chassis. The existing bore and stroke measurements of 9.6 and 11.3 litre units were retained, but metric references were discontinued and these new power units were known by their approximate imperial cubic inches capacities. These were AV590 and AV690 respectively. It was something of a contradiction because AEC still quoted bore and stroke dimensions in millimetres. In the new order of things 'V' represented vertical engine; and there were horizontal (H) versions for passenger chassis applications. Industrial engines were also available along with turbo-charged versions for specialised automotive applications overseas, railcars, and high power stationary engine requirements.

AV590 and AV690 engines were completely different designs from 9.6 and 11.3 litre types. They were based on wet liner A410/A470 units introduced in 1953 for AEC Mercurys and Reliances. (See *The AEC Mercury*). Wet liner engines offered better cooling capability because coolant was in direct contact with all of the liner, although cylinder blocks tended to be less rigid. These engines were also assembled from monobloc castings, which are cylinder blocks and crankcases comprising one composite casting rather than separate components, as was previously established AEC practise. Such designs resulted in lower manufacturing costs and AEC had invested heavily in new engine production machinery. Other traditional AEC engine characteristics were retained, however, such as masked inlet valves, and toroidal cavity combustion chambers machined into piston crowns to cause high velocity swirling of induced air for efficient fuel combustion and instant starting. Early AV590 and AV690 engines had in-line fuel injection pumps supplied by either Simms or CAV, and multi-hole injectors, which were housed in copper sheaths in contact with the coolant. There were two interchangeable cylinder heads with each covering three cylinders.

When the first AEC Mandator Mk.Vs entered service in 1959 engine outputs were identical to the 9.6 and 11.3 litre units they superseded. For the AV590, 125 bhp at 1,800 rpm, with 430 lbs. ft. of torque at 1,000 rpm, and the AV690 produced 150 bhp at 1,800 rpm, with 505 lbs. ft. torque at 1,100 rpm.

A single, hydraulically operated dry plate clutch of 262 square inches frictional area was unit mounted with the engine and gearbox. A clutch brake was also fitted for quick and clean gear changing with the 5-speed direct drive top constant mesh gearbox. Alternatively, and frequently, a 6-speed overdrive version of the same unit could be specified. Various power take-offs could also be fitted if the lorry was used for tipping or pumping work.

Completing the driveline was a tough, double reduction, spiral bevel double helical back axle with fully floating half shafts. Standard differential ratio was 6.22:1 with alternatives of 7.12:1 and 7.92:1. This gearing was not fitted with an AV690 engine and top speed of a Mandator Mk.V with 6-speed gearbox, and lowest axle ratio was approximately 50 mph on 9.00 x 20 tyres. Export vehicles generally had 11.00 x 20 covers and many British operators actually specified 10.00 x 20 tyres for an extra margin of tolerance and safety for prolonged Motorway running.

Mandator Mk.Vs had a newly designed chassis 10 inches deep by 3 inches flange width fabricated from steel slightly more than ½ inch thick. The front axle was retracted, or set back, for better loading tolerances and this feature also allowed easier access to the cab for the driver because a lower step could be sited ahead of the wheel. An attractive and stylish range of cabs was proposed for all AEC Mk.V's and Southall's draughtsmen provided plans to several coach builders who diligently followed these blueprints, which included provision for heating and demisting equipment. Some cab manufacturers, such as Duramin used aluminium alloy throughout the structures. Chassis still left Southall with only a front scuttle in place.

These lorries had lighter and cheaper radiators than early Mk.IIIs with film blocks being used. Traditional worm and nut steering boxes were retained and hydraulic power assistance was available at extra cost. Semi-elliptic multi-leaf springs were used on both axles and a 48 gallons capacity fuel tank was fitted.

Mandator Mk.Vs gained reputations for possessing excellent brakes, and a full air pressure system was used. Single leading shoe, cam operated assemblies with worm wheel slack adjusters acted in brake drums 4¾ inches wide at the front and 7¾ inches wide at the rear. With drums of 15½ inches diameter the total braking area was 746 square inches. To guard against total braking failure a divided air pressure system could be ordered. An exhaust brake to assist the foundation brakes was also optional. A ratchet type mechanical hand brake acted upon the rear shoes for parking purposes.

All vehicles in AEC's Mk.V series were designed as a family with common components for parts interchangeability. This caused Mandators and Mammoth Majors to be popular with fleet operators whose maintenance fitters could easily familiarise themselves with different models within the range. Also, storekeepers could order and stock fewer spare parts.

In the year 1962, with sales growing steadily, higher power engines were introduced for Mandator Mk.V lorries. By then the Motorway network was rapidly expanding and operators were demanding even greater horsepower. Consequently, AV590 and AV690 engines were uprated and crankshaft vibration dampers were fitted to guard against bottom end failures. It had been discovered that non-dampened crankshafts could knock out big ends at flat out running over many miles of Motorways.

These re-tuned and modified power units were prefixed with the figure '2', and the 2AV590 produced 158 bhp at 2,000 rpm. The 2AV690 was capable of 192 bhp, also at 2,000 rpm, and newly introduced CAV DPA fuel injection pumps were normally fitted. These were also known as rotary, or distributor type fuel pumps. Torque outputs were also correspondingly higher at 480 and 560 lbs. ft. respectively.

The following year, 1963, saw several revisions to Mandator Mk.V specifications. All new chassis received a '2' prefix, becoming 2G4RA series lorries. The 2AV690 engine became the standard fitment and if metric brake horsepower figures were quoted AEC was able to claim an output of 200 bhp at 2,000 rpm. This made a Mandator Mk.V tractive unit, along with a Leyland Beaver, one of the most powerful lorries in the 24 tons gross weight category available in Great Britain. Further engine developments had improved fuel consumption and reliability. A newly designed 6-speed constant mesh overdrive gearbox was also fitted along with a modified rear axle with lighter hubs. A heavy-duty back axle was also available for heavy haulage and export market Mandators.

All '2 series' Mandator Mk.Vs received re-designed braking assemblies for improved efficiency. Previously with AEC designed components, there were incidences of rapid lining wear, brake fading with continuous use, and cracking brake drums. The improved components sourced from Girling alleviated these problems. Screw type brake shoe adjusters were used and front linings were now 5 inches wide. Those at the rear were slightly narrower than before at 7 inches wide. A variable ratio mechanical hand brake with air assistance replaced the multiple pull, ratchet type. With even better brakes, '2 series' Mandator Mk.V tractive units would comfortably qualify for uprating to 30 tons gross vehicle weight after the new Construction and Use Regulations were implemented in 1965. All that was required was further modification to 3-line trailer braking and fitting multi-diaphragm brake chambers. A "dead man" emergency control handle and additional air reservoir were also needed. These alterations were satisfactory for interim braking standards introduced for Annual Testing and Plating in 1968, and also qualified for final braking requirements in 1972. Unmodified G4RA and 2G4RA Mandators still met interim braking standards for 24 tons gross weight operations.

A deeper and wider chassis frame was also used for these Mandators. The depth was increased by 2 inches and the width by ¼ inch. To save some weight the steel was ⅛ inch thinner than before. To provide smoother riding characteristics hydraulic dampers were fitted on the front axle to assist the leaf springs.

A special drawbar prime mover Mandator Mk.V was specifically designed for export markets where 36 tons train weights were the norm. It was built on a 15 feet 1 inch wheelbase with heavy-duty rear axle. Also for certain countries such as South Africa, a passenger-carrying version of a Mandator Mk.V was available. It was named Kudu and in spite of AEC producing a comprehensive range of passenger chassis, none were deemed suitable for operating regularly across rough terrain and rudimentary roads. With all AEC bus and coach designs by the early 1960s having either low chassis, or under floor engines, or a combination of both, a modified, rugged lorry chassis gave greater tolerances.

Since the introduction of Mandator Mk.Vs in 1959, sales of tractive units had been growing, and the vast majority of these AECs were purchased for articulated lorry duties. When improved '2 series' versions were produced from 1963, Mandator Mk.Vs cemented their reputation as market leaders. Many hauliers placed Mandators into service in the early 1960s, including BRS, which operated several hundred of them. However, by summer 1965 Mandator Mk.Vs were being phased out in readiness for yet another modernised version. The last Mk.Vs entered service in 1966 and usually had newly introduced AV691 engines fitted.

*Clelland must have been satisfied with is Matador back in 1933, because in early 1961 it was still buying AECs, and this Mandator Mk.V was on contract to Caledonian Cement. They were still hauling the same commodity, but by then bulk deliveries were commonplace. (Negative 21592)*

*One of those legendary Caterpillar D8 machines being moved to a new site by Cransford's Mandator Mk.V. The Cat's blade is on the neck of the trailer. It was quite legal to do such work on trade plates back in 1961. (Negative 21870)*

*There's a good load on Allison's Mandator and BTC four-in-line trailer, and it has been expertly sheeted and roped by its driver who was finishing off at the back. Allison's appeared not to specify bumper bars on its AECs. The gentleman in the overcoat and homburg hat is unknown, but the location is thought to have been a foundry adjacent to London Road, Glasgow. (Negative 21858)*

*Most Mandators for drawbar trailer duties were exported, as by the late 1950s such '2-axle plus 2-axle' combinations were being seen less frequently here in Great Britain. This petroleum tanker and trailer outfit was in service in South Africa with B.P. (Negative A28743)*

*A fine trio of Mandator Mk.V rigids with boxvan trailers destined for an unrecorded overseas destination. They were designed for capacity rather than maximum weight, judging by the use of single rear wheels on the back axles. Also, their cabs had doors suspended on the rear pillars, a style favoured by coachbuilders RTS, and fondly remembered as "suicide doors". (Negative A25958)*

*Working hard for its keep in South Africa in the service of Hume Concrete Pipes. A Mandator being used as an 'A Train', that is pulling two trailers; the first being articulated and the second being either a drawbar or an articulated trailer on a dolly. The overall length was approximately seventy feet, but the mirrors were rather small for observing following traffic. (Negative A24010)*

*A genuine working shot of Tancock's Mandator and ubiquitous four-in-line trailer in 1962. It was extremely rare to carry bricks as a part load, even though there was not much on the front of the trailer. That poorly sheeted consignment with sacks hoping to keep the goods dry was probably returns from a customer and then the driver would have filled out with a back load of bricks. Look at the dents in the wings of the AEC and trailer. (Negative 25991)*

*On the A40 at Beaconsfield in 1962, probably going to or from home in South Wales. A fine shot, typical of 1960s trucking. It is safe to assume that Davies' trailer was supplied by York Trailer Co. (Negative 27070)*

*Shell-Mex and B.P. Ltd. was one of the big Mandator Mk.V fleets. They were always beautifully turned out vehicles, as befitted their status as the largest petroleum products distributor. At the time experiments were being carried with reverse fifth wheel couplings, with king pin on the tractive unit and the plate and jaws on the trailer. (Negative 26251)*

*Midland Motor Co. was an Allison's Freightlines subsidiary company and this Mandator was used on a regular night trunk between Nottingham and Glasgow, running north with loads from British Gypsum at East Leake, and returning south with steel. Neil Mitchell, my collaborator on this series of books used to shunt this lorry during the day. (Negative 35655)*

*A fascinating double four-in-line trailer behind the Mex Mandator Mk.V drawbar lorry in Ireland. Both tanks were discharging at the same time and the man on top was attempting to check the dips. (Negative 27270)*

*Mobil was another big user of Mandator Mk.V's and favoured four-in-line tank trailers of 4,000 gallons capacity. Mobil was originally the Vacuum Oil Company, noted for the quality of its lubricants, and did not begin retailing petrol in this country until it commissioned Coryton refinery in 1954. Mobil became part of BP in 1997. (Negative 23167)*

*Adams Butter had its main creamery and factory at Leek and ran several Mandator Mk.V artics on trunking duties. Typically for the period they were coupled to four-in-line trailers with special boxvan bodies. Atypically, some of these Mandators were prototypes for evaluating sustained fast Motorway running on recently opened stretches of the M1 in the early '60s. They were fitted with non-standard, high-speed diffs, and engines that were higher revving than normal with special low friction pistons.*

*The well-known timber merchants of E. Whatton & Sons Ltd. placed this Mandator Mk.V into service in 1965. It also had a new pole trailer, with massive super single tyres. These were very rare back then and the idea of a puncture away from base must have been frightening. It also had unusual bar grip tyres on the drive axle to aid off road traction, but tyre wear on normal roads would have been excessive. (Negative 33713)*

*Nicol of Coatbridge was another well-remembered Scottish haulier. Back in 1963 it was hauling pipes from Stewart & Lloyds at Mossend, Lanarkshire on over length trailers for indivisible loads. The pipes were used for constructing a national gas grid that would eventually be used for distributing North Sea gas in the next decade. This storage area was at Luton Gas Works. (Negative 28242)*

*Air Products is the British subsidiary of an American corporation. It only began producing gasses here as late as 1959, but subsequent growth was exceptional. The company bought its first Mandator in 1962, which was then followed by another twenty-two Mk.Vs. This one, chassis number 2G4RA 1723 entered service on 1st January 1965 and was returning from Belgium by cross-channel ferry when photographed. It was coupled to a frameless liquefied gas tanker trailer. (Photo: Air Products)*

*Hanson of Huddersfield was an AEC user of long-standing, dating back to the early 1930s. By the mid-1960s it had several prestigious contracts with lorries liveried to the requirements of customers. One such contract was with ICI Dyestuffs Division and this late 1965 Mandator Mk.V was taking advantage of the new C. &. U. Regs. by being coupled to a new maximum length 33-foot tanker trailer.*
*(Photo: J. Morris Bray / Author's collection)*

*Since this night-time exposure picture was made in 1964, Birmingham's famous Bull Ring has been completely re-built again. Back then it was relatively modern, having been re-designed for the first time. An Mk.V Mandator of Carborundum from Trafford Park, Manchester was on a night trunk run to the company's Birmingham depot. Typical of the period, it was coupled to a BTC four-in-line trailer.*
*(Photo: Author's collection, source unknown)*

*This was originally a Mandator Mk.V that was still in service as late as 1991 in Australia. It had left Southall nearly thirty years previously and was converted to 6x4 layout in the parent company's workshops (R.W. Brown & Co). Later it was re-engined with an AV760 unit and 15-speed Fuller compound 'two-stick' gearbox. It worked in Brown's Newcastle Haulage and Transport division. (Photo: Tony Petch)*

*By the early 1960s AEC was winning significant sales in Europe, and particularly in the Benelux countries. Cabs were usually built locally and this Mandator was equipped with an attractively styled sleeper cab made by Bollekens. Tilt bodied drawbar combinations were the mainstays of long distance European haulage then. (Photo: Arthur Ingram)*

*A magnificent picture of Rockbank Transport's Mandator Mk.V about to take to the roads for the first time. Again it was a long wheelbase tractor unit and with an extra, non-AEC fuel tank for long distance. The locally assembled cab, probably by Hastings Deering, had a sleeper shelf, and the Fruehauf trailer appeared to have been imported from the U.S.A. It was typical American practice of that era to have them unpainted bright aluminium alloy, with rearmost positioned bogie.*
*(Photo: Peter Mendoza Studios from Tony Petch)*

*Thomas Nationwide Transport – TNT – became a worldwide name in Transport in the latter quarter of the twentieth century. This stunning picture of a Mandator Mk.V was taken outside the company's premises in Sydney. Note the longer wheelbase of the Mandator for the Australian market.*
*(Photo: Young & Richardson from Tony Petch)*

*Even though AEC had a successful range of specialised Mammoth Major based Dumptruks, there was a demand for smaller site lorries and short wheelbase Mandators were suitable for working in demanding conditions both on and off road. Aberdeen Council had some Mandator Mk.III dumpers and in 1963 bought some Mk.V versions, one of each being captured working with a Ruston Bucyrus excavator. (Negative C29289)*

*A lovely nostalgic close-up of a lorry and cargo that epitomised British general haulage of the 1960s. J. &. A. Smith of Madiston, a famous name and major fleet of the time. A Mandator Mk.V and four-in-line trailer, one of the most popular artic combinations. The driver "hand balling" a load of cartons of aluminium foil, expertly stacked. Once loaded it had to be securely sheeted and roped. Back then there was a lot more to lorry driving than merely sitting behind a steering wheel. Great memories! (Negative C30313)*

*By the early 1960s Harold Wood was introducing articulated lorries into his very large AEC fleet that until then was entirely rigids. Mandator Mk.Vs were chosen with over 50 in service by 1964 and a further 79 on order. By then unaccompanied tank trailers were being sent to the continent, and this Mandator Mk.V had collected a European trailer from the "Dorric Ferry" at Tilbury. (Negative C30296)*

*AEC's were popular in Eire for many years, being assembled locally from CKD units at Dundalk. Whilst this is obviously a posed photo it does show a rarity to non-Irish readers, namely a full load of turf, or peat, used for fuel. The Mandator Mk.V and trailer was in service with McHenry Bros Ltd. in 1962. (Negative C28693)*

# SECTION 4

## Ergomatic Cabbed Mandators

AEC Mandator Mk.Vs, and in particular '2 series' models, were destined to have a relatively short production run. This was not because of any fundamental design weaknesses, but simply due to the hectic pace of change in the 1960s. Coincidental with the expansion of Motorway and fast dual carriageway trunk route networks, vast tonnages of goods were also transferring onto roads from the railways. There were two reasons for this; firstly rail fright had been uncompetitive for decades, and as road journey times became shorter it prompted thousands of manufacturing businesses to transfer their transport and distribution to hauliers. Secondly, when Dr. Beeching implemented his infamous railway closures, road transport received another tremendous boost. Parallel to this unprecedented growth, revolutionary legislation contained in the 1964 Construction and Use Regulations demanded considerably improved vehicles from manufacturers. Articulated lorries in particular gained most from the statutes, being granted a potential for 32 tons gross weight, which was an increase of 8 tons (or 33.3%) over the old limit. Quite simply, it was a period when neither lorry builders nor operators could stagnate and modern designs were urgently needed.

When the striking Ergomatic cabbed range of AECs was unveiled at the Commercial Vehicle Show in 1964, AEC was able to capitalise on the success it was enjoying with its lorries. Mandators contained some features from 2G4R Mk.V models, but they were updated in most respects. One obvious change was the use of a Leyland Motors Group tilting cab designed in Italy at the studios of Giovanni Michelotti and manufactured in England by Joseph Sankey, (later GKN Sankey). AEC, Albion, and Leyland shared this driver's structure and it was the first tangible sign of Leyland's growing influence in Southall's affairs. Incidentally, there is now evidence to suggest that shortly after the 1962 merger between ACV (AEC's parent holding company) and Leyland Motors, AEC instigated the initial development of a totally new tilting cab, and Leyland then took over this project. It has always been believed that the Ergomatic cab was purely a Leyland Motors venture. Without doubt, both companies were badly in need of more driver friendly cabs in the early 1960s. The Ergomatic cab has been fully described in other titles within "The Commercial Vehicles Archive Series."

It was almost twelve months after the autumn 1964 Commercial Motor Show before the first new Mandators entered service. Chassis designations were TG4R or L, with T indicating tilting cab, R and L for right or left hand control respectively. As a solo lorry a Mandator was now able to operate at the recently implemented maximum four wheeler gross weight of 16 tons, and three load carrier wheelbases of 12 feet 1 inch, 15 feet 0 inches, and 18 feet 0 inches were available. With a drawbar trailer the gross train weight was 32 tons, or 36 tons for export versions with heavy-duty back axles. Such was the pro-articulated lorry bias of latest legislation that for the home market Ergomatic cabbed Mandators were mainly tractive units of 9 feet 6 inches wheelbase. Gross train weights were 30, or 32 tons with the tractor rated at 15 tons; 5 tons front axle and 10 tons rear. Overseas models were designed for 36 tons train weights.

The 1964 legislation was quirky with regards to top gross weight limits, and two categories were quoted because overall vehicle length limits permitted a maximum semi-trailer length of 33 feet. With what is easiest described as a "standard" 33-foot trailer, 30 tons gross weight was comfortably attainable, allowing about 20.5 tons payload. To achieve the articulated lorry maximum of 32 tons on four axles required the trailer's rear bogie to be at the extremity of its chassis, which in turn made legal axle weight loadings virtually impossible. The implications of this will be discussed further in Section 5.

Not only were TG4 Mandators visually modern, they also contained several interesting mechanical developments. Power was from an AV691 engine, which was a further progression of the AV690. For this modified unit, AEC reverted to dry cylinder liners and re-designed the cylinder heads. Bore and stroke dimensions were unchanged as were those of the crankshaft journals, but revised engine timings were introduced. The crankshaft was made from a special steel alloy and was nitride hardened for long operational service. A CAV DPA rotary fuel injection pump was retained for a maximum, optional, output of 205 bhp at 2,200 rpm and torque of 573 lbs. ft. at 1,200 rpm. The standard setting was for 187 bhp at 2,200 rpm and 544 lbs. ft. of torque. If even more power was demanded either Simms or CAV in-line pumps could be specified for a maximum rating of 218 bhp.

However, by early 1966, if an operator needed such power, a bored out version of the AV691 became available. With a bore of 136 mm (5.37 inches) and stroke of 142 mm (5.59 inches) an AV760 engine, as the new unit was designated, produced up to 226 bhp at 2,200 rpm, with 618 lbs. ft. torque at 1,500 rpm. The swept volume of the unit was 12,473 cubic centimetres, or 761 cubic inches. Initially either Simms or CAV in-line fuel injection pumps were fitted, but later a third injection pump option, namely Bosch, became available. The standard AV760 power setting was 206 bhp at 2,000 rpm and 588 lbs. ft. of torque at 1,500 rpm. Maximum output was available as an option at home and it was standard overseas. In subsequent years when AV760 engines were AEC's front line large capacity power units, a de-rated version with CAV DPA rotary pump was also produced for certain applications such as Marshal Majors. (See *The AEC Mustang & Marshal)*. However, in 1966 an AEC Mandator with AV760 engine producing 226 bhp was the most powerful maximum weight, general purpose, articulated lorry available in Great Britain. These latest AEC engines were also available in horizontal format for passenger chassis installations, and as vertical marine or industrial power units.

Early tilt cabbed Mandator tractive units were made to a 'standard' specification for operating at 30 tons gross train weight. AV691 engines at 187 bhp were fitted and drive was through a 16 inches diameter friction plate clutch that was operated hydraulically with air assistance. Unit mounted to the clutch and engine was a D203 6-speed constant mesh overdrive gearbox, and the driveline was completed by a double reduction, spiral bevel double helical back axle. Four ratios were available and the standard was 6.25:1. Options were 5.67:1, 7.08:1, and 7.89:1. With normal ratio the lorry's top speed was about 56 mph on 10.00 x 20 tyres. Various other tyre sizes could be specified; 9.00 x 24, 11.00 x 20, 11.00 x 22, or 9.00 x 20.

Interestingly, all AEC tilt cabbed lorries were originally planned for 11.00 x 20 tyres and cab front wings had radii to accommodate such covers. However, tyre manufacturers up-rated 10.00 x 20 sizes to 16-ply rating, which complied with new legal requirements, so bigger (and heavier) tyres were strictly unnecessary. If alternative tyre sizes were ordered as options a different front axle to that normally fitted was recommended. British haulage contractors preferred 16-ply, 10.00 x 20 tyres because they were lighter and cheaper than larger sizes.

For heavier loads and faster speeds more efficient brakes were provided, with 6 inches wide front brake shoes and 8 inches wide rear ones. The 15½ inches diameter brake drums were ribbed for additional strength and better cooling. Total braking area was 832 square inches. Actuation was by full air pressure and assemblies were single leading shoe cam expanded types. An air assisted mechanical handbrake was provided for parking purposes, and this acted on the rear wheels only. To comply with new braking regulations 3-line trailer brakes were provided with a "dead man" handle for emergency braking. This opened a valve which operated the Mandator's front axle brakes and those of the trailer. The air circuit was a split system and a dual foot valve fed separate tractor and trailer circuits. Independent reservoirs supplied air to multiple diaphragm brake actuators, the hand brake, and clutch.

These early Ergomatic Mandator tractor units had chassis frames 9¼ inches deep by 2½ inches wide fabricated from steel just over ¼ inch thick. Load carriers had stronger frames of 12 inches deep by 3 inches wide. The front of the chassis frame was cranked to permit a low cab height. This in turn allowed easy entry into the driver's structure courtesy of a single step positioned ahead of the front wheel. Fixed to the nearside chassis rail was a 48 gallons capacity fuel tank as standard, but a more capacious 75 gallons tank could be supplied. Later, this became the usual fitting.

Long, flexible, semi-elliptic multi-leaf springs were used front and rear and telescopic hydraulic dampers assisted those on the front axle. The lorry's steering was by recirculatory ball, worm and nut. Hydraulic power assistance was optional for tractive units and standard for longer wheelbase models.

It had long been AEC's policy to offer its customers a base specification that could be amended to order, and advertising a 'standard' Mandator was unusual for the company. In fact, when AV760 engines became available in mid-1966, the 'standard' tag was soon dropped. Within a couple of years the more powerful engine had become the popular choice with operators and the AV691 alternative was eventually discontinued in lorries. There were operational problems with AV691 engines fitted in Mandators and Mammoth Majors. They were prone to serious overheating caused partly by the thickness of cylinder liners, and also by poor cooling characteristics of Ergomatic cabs. (See Section 6). If an AV760 engine was specified then a larger diameter clutch of 17 inches was provided. Even when the 'standard' label was applied some options were listed, including exhaust brake, various power take offs, and heavy-duty back axle. The standard ratio of this component was 6.22:1, and alternatives were 5.85:1, 2.12:1, and 7.92:1.

Typically, in 1966, a Mandator tractor with fifth wheel and all equipment weighed 5 tons 4 hundredweights. A 33-foot tandem axle trailer made to a lightweight design by such as York, Scammell, or Boden was approximately 4 tons 4 hundredweights, giving a total combined unladen weight of a shade under 9½ tons. Therefore at 30 tons gross weight a legal payload of 20½ tons was possible, which was almost 3 tons more than a 26 tons gross weight eight-wheeler. Not many rigid eights were built for operating at this newly introduced weight category because they were long and awkward to manoeuvre. (Refer to *The Leyland Octopus)*. With an articulated lorry and trailer also being cheaper to buy it is hardly surprising that such combinations soon became very popular. This advantage was even more pronounced later in 1966 when all Mandator tractive units were for 32 tons train weight, although a tri-axle trailer was the only practical means of achieving this. Even so, a legal payload of approximately 22 tons was a mouth-watering prospect for transport company bosses. It was not until 1968 that a revision of axle spread dimensions and an increase in overall length limits comfortably permitted 32 tons gross weight on four axles for articulated lorries.

Long wheelbase Mandator load carriers weighed some 6½ tons empty with flat platform body and as 16 tonners could carry 9½ tons. If used with a drawbar trailer the overall payload was approximately 20 tons. Some Mandator rigids, mainly for export, were rated for 14 tons gross weight.

In mid-1966 E.L. Cornwell, Technical Editor of 'Modern Transport', tested an AEC Mandator demonstrator. The lorry was an artic and powered by an AV760 engine. It had a non-standard back axle ratio of 7.08:1 which gave a top speed of 47 mph. It was coupled to a 32-foot Scammell tandem axle semi-trailer and the combination grossed 29 tons 18 hundredweights for a payload of exactly 20½ tons. The tester subjected the Mandator to a 108 miles route that encompassed a variety of single and dual carriageway roads in southern suburban London, and Motorways along the Surrey and Kent borders. Mr. Cornwell was very impressed with this lorry finding it to be "quiet, extremely comfortable, and untiring to drive." He thought that it "executed a big job with a minimum of stress and strain," with the Ergomatic cab being "convenient." The clutch action and gear changing was first rate. The AEC's exhaust was clean under all driving conditions; braking was "good and consistent," the stable suspension gave a pleasant laden ride, and the steering was light with "no need for power assistance."

A short stretch of Motorway was used and 44 mph average speed attained at a "remarkable" 8.8 mpg. On a lengthy hilly section fuel consumption fell to 6.4 mpg and the average speed was 26 mph. Mr Cornwell was generally very impressed with the Mandator and thought it "handsome and easy to manage." He left it "feeling as fresh as when he started." His only recommendation was for a higher rear axle to be fitted for Motorway running, for which the standard 6.25:1 gearing was eminently suitable. List price for this AV760 engined Mandator ready for the road was £4,329 in 1966, and the test trailer was £1,600. Total outfit price was £5,929 for 20½ tons payload. "Better value would be hard to find," commented Mr. Cornwell.

Notwithstanding teething problems with what was to all intents and purposes a brand new model, sales of Ergomatic cabbed Mandators rocketed as both own account and hire and reward operators clamoured for articulated lorries. By the end of 1966 orders for troublesome AV691 powered Mandators were a tiny minority as more powerful AV760 engines were preferred. This power unit gained a great reputation for reliability and longevity; Ergomatic cabs were very popular with drivers, Mandators were fast with good hill climbing characteristics, and had excellent brakes. In short, AEC had produced a market-leading lorry.

By the late 1960s articulated lorries had usurped eight-wheelers as heavyweight flagships for most road haulage tasks. AEC Mandators had developed into thoroughly reliable, productive, and profitable lorries. During the first three years or so of Ergomatic cabbed models AEC had acted upon feedback from operators and rectified any shortcomings. Various improvements had also been incorporated into the design to take into account the fact that after 1968 the majority of Mandators constantly worked at 32 tons gross weights. Stronger chassis frames were used for tractive units, with dimensions of 10 inches by 3 inches and this added a couple of hundredweights to the unladen weight. A slightly heavier front axle had also been fitted and for load tolerance was rated at 5.35 tons. From 1970, wider front springs of 4 inches could also be specified as alternatives in place of standard 3 inches wide ones.

There was a change of manufacturing policy enforced onto AEC by Leyland that did cause a few problems in 1967-8. This was the introduction of Butec electrical components such as alternators, starter motors, and control units. Leyland Motors began manufacturing these items under the Butec name to combat a perceived monopoly of supply enjoyed by CAV and Simms. Butec parts were made from designs supplied under licence from Leece-Neville of Ohio, and initially with these were not sufficiently robust or entirely suitable for British operating conditions. Modifications were necessary and thereafter Butec components generally became reliable.

Another useful optional extra was an air operated cross axle difflock for the rear axle to combat tricky road surface conditions in winter. All Mandator tractors were now equipped with load sensing valves in braking systems and this regulated the effort of the driving axle brakes. This prevented the brakes locking the wheels if the trailer was not fully loaded. When driving wheels did lock-up it was the main cause of jack knifing by artics because the back axle became a pivot about which the trailer could turn as it continued to push against the tractor. Load sensing valves were a cheap and effective means of reducing incidences of jack knifing.

In the year 1969 two new, additional gearboxes became available as options. To provide extra ratios an AEC 10-speed splitter unit could be fitted. This was basically the same 5-speed gearbox as the standard constant mesh unit, but the overdrive sixth speed was replaced by an air-operated splitter (half) gear, which then provided overdrive for each main ratio. Alternatively, the Leyland Pneumo-Cyclic semi-automatic transmission could be fitted. This consisted of five main ratios and an air-operated splitter to provide a total of ten ratios and was identical to that used for Leyland 'Two-Pedal Beavers' as described in *The Leyland Beaver*. Mandators with such gearboxes did not have clutch pedals. Either of these multi-ratio gearboxes gave a final top speed similar to that achieved with a standard 6-speed overdrive unit, but provided drivers with more flexibility on hills.

Both optional transmissions were also used in some AEC Mandator V8 chassis, and this was a completely different Mandator model introduced in 1968. The development and in-service history of the short-lived Mandator V8 tractive unit was studied in *AEC Mandator V8*, published in 1997 and now out of print.

Into the early 1970s and AEC Mandators remained popular with both hire and reward and own account fleet operators. However, the invasion of Scandinavian and European tractive units was gathering pace as drivers and transport managers recognised the superior comfort offered by these imported lorries. Mechanically they offered similar power to top British models such as Mandators, but multi-ratio gearboxes and power assisted steering also came as standard specification from such as Volvo and Scania.

In the year 1971 AEC revised its Mandator chassis designation by prefixing the model type with a '2'. This signified a repositioned radiator header tank, which was moved from under the engine cover to the rear of the cab. It also increased the coolant capacity of the system and was welcomed by Mandator purchasers. In this same year the Pneumo-Cyclic semi-automatic gearbox was discontinued because it had proved troublesome in service and the reasons are given in *The Leyland Beaver*. Not many Mandators had been supplied with this particular optional transmission, but in its place AEC offered another 10-speed gearbox which was its own design of constant mesh range change unit. Within twelve months the alternative AEC splitter gearbox was dropped, but still leaving prospective purchasers with a choice of either 6-speed, or 10-speed gearboxes. By 1974 the AEC range change gearbox was de-listed and was replaced by a bought-in 9-speed constant mesh Fuller Roadranger range change unit.

Because AEC and Leyland group customers were ordering only relatively small numbers of these optional units, it was cheaper to purchase range change transmissions from such as Eaton-Fuller who supplied truck builders worldwide.

As the 1970s progressed British Leyland, as the parent organisation had become by then, was in worsening financial plight and industrial relations in its car manufacturing subsidiaries was dire. The relatively successful commercial vehicle plants were forced to subsidise other company divisions and capital for further development of models such as Mandators was non-existent. AEC had blotted its copybook with its Mandator V8 failure, and Leyland was experiencing monumental difficulties with fixed head 500 Series engines and the lorries they powered. The Scandinavians and Europeans had made substantial in-roads into British fleets and in response AEC was directed to design and develop the Leyland Marathon premium specification range. This important model will be examined in a subsequent "Commercial Vehicles Archive Series" book.

By 1975 senior Leyland executives were keen to halt Mandator production and replace it with a choice of newer models for clients. These were either the Marathon, or the 500 Series Leyland Buffalo. However, AEC customers had always shown tremendous loyalty and some of these, such as major oil companies, had plenty of clout. Haulage fleets including Jempsons of Rye, and Willmotts of Wells also continued to place orders. This ensured that Mandators remained in production, although by the mid-seventies the model was becoming dated. Some cosmetic changes were introduced to cab grilles, but that was about all.

In the year 1977 Leyland Motors belatedly embarked on a model rationalisation programme that would ultimately lead to AEC being axed as both a marque and manufacturing division. Ironically, Leyland also had to abandon its 500 series engine programme as warranty claims became unsustainable and the company's reputation was in tatters. An alternative engine offered in Buffalos to replace the Leyland 511 was a Leyland L12, which was developed from AEC's AV760. This was basically a normally aspirated version of the turbo-charged TL12 as used in Leyland Marathons and, from 1981 for a time, Leyland T45 Roadtrains. A Leyland Buffalo L12 tractive unit also had an AEC D203 6-speed gearbox and was virtually an AEC Mandator by another name.

The last AEC Mandator built was chassis number 2TG4R 36,214 and it was completed at Southall on 5th July 1977. After being stored by a dealer for several months it entered service registered YNG 181S on 1st June 1978 with Alcocks Transport of Kings Lynn. It is rumoured to have survived into preservation with a Scottish collector, but this has not been confirmed.

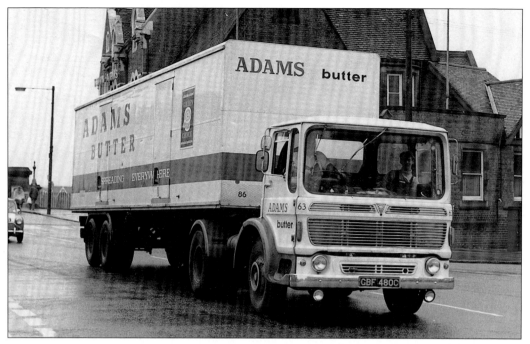

*An interesting photo of one of Adams Butter Mandators, first registered in 1965, although the shot was taken some years later. The AEC had received a newer, re-styled bottom grille panel and bumper bar, but its mirror arms were still located in their original positions on the doors. Mirrors in this location were notorious for easily becoming dirty because of road spray swirling onto them. Tilt-cabs had poor aerodynamics. (NegativeA44016)*

*An immaculately sheeted and roped load representative of general haulage in the mid-1960s. Willmotts of Wells ran Mk.V Mandators then purchased some of the first TG models in 1965. They also bought some of the very last Mandators made in 1977. Were roads really so deserted forty years ago? Savour this evocative, nostalgic picture; scenes like this will never occur again. (Negative A34947)*

Tunnel Cement was a long-standing AEC customer and placed some innovative articulated outfits in service in 1966. Based on AV691 powered Mandators the tanks were lightweight frameless designs fabricated from aluminium alloy by Bonallack. The train weight was 28 tons for a payload of 18 tons of cement. Trailer running gear was by Crane Freuhauf and tank discharge was by a compressor driven through a full torque power take-off. (Negative A34669)

AEC stalwart Harold Wood soon ordered tilt-cabbed Mandators and his 1966 example was on contract to Berk Chemicals with a new maximum length 33-foot acid tanker. By then Wood had over four hundred AECs in his fleet and was rapidly switching to articulated lorries, having bought his first ones only four years previously. The statutory three-line air braking system is clearly visible for compliance with the 1965 C. & U. Regs. (Negative A34928)

*Bulk Powders (Midlands) Ltd. was a Nottingham based firm specifically founded to specialise in what its name said. A relatively new and small concern in 1966 it ordered AEC Mandators for its operations with high capacity food grade tank trailers for commodities such as flour and starch. This was an innovative trailer built by Neville of Mansfield on Nord running gear. The rear bogie could be brought forward for weighing on short weighbridges, so obviating the need for split combination weighing. Was the driver aware that his diesel tank cap was open? (Negative A35643)*

*This was how the A74 at Beattock used to be shortly after it was made into a dual carriageway in the mid-sixties and almost devoid of traffic. The Mandator was owned by James Hemphill of Glasgow and was on contract to ICI Salt Division. By then many different types of powder were transported in bulk. In the case of common salt it was purely for convenience; being such a cheap commodity the financial savings for the customer by buying in bulk were minimal. (Negative A38970)*

*This was an innovative design of trailer to capitalise on the maximum 32 tons weight on five axles. Conceived by Associated British Maltsters it comprised a Mandator and tri-axle trailer which was built by Murfitt and had a moving bulkhead for discharging its load. The running gear was by Schmitz, a name virtually unknown in Great Britain back then, and had a self-steering bogie. Axles one and three both steered. Whilst this would provide excellent manoeuvrability when going forward, reversing it successfully would have taken practice. (Negative A34955)*

*By 1967 most of the new Mandator's teething problems had been eradicated and they were building a reputation for reliability. One important improvement and modification had been made to the tilt-cab's locking mechanism with screw-in bolts being introduced. It had been discovered that with the original locking system the cab could tilt under heavy braking and there was a least one recorded driver fatality because of this. This pair of Mandators was Hanson lorries, on contract to Castrol. (Photo: J. Morris Bray)*

*A load of paper, probably imported brown reels from Scandinavia, for converting into packaging. In the mid-sixties the port of Manchester was thriving, but within a few short years containerisation would bring about its demise. The Mandator was owned by Manchester Ship Canal Company (Bridgewater Estates) and it has survived to the present day in preservation. (Negative A35168)*

*By 1967 when this Mandator in the livery of Beefeater Gin entered service the containerisation revolution was gathering pace. Many hauliers were ill-prepared and resorted to carrying ISO containers on standard trailers rather than dedicated skeletal units with twist locks for retaining the box. It can be seen that only ordinary ropes were holding this container, a highly dangerous practice that resulted in more than one unfortunate driver being killed when his load shot forward under heavy braking conditions. Also in shot at Burroughs's London distillery was a BRS AEC Mercury tractive unit with a very early curtain sided trailer. (Negative A37988)*

*There was a long tipping trailer behind Hampshire County Council's Mandator used for collecting road stone from quarries for use on the county's roads. Most artic tippers were shorter than this, but for 32 tons gross weight on four axles maximum outer axle spread dimensions had to be adhered to.*
*(Negative A41270)*

*4/12. Founded in 1949 by Spalding farmer George Machin, the road haulage company that bore his name expanded in the fifties and sixties under the direction of 'Captain' (or Jack) Garn. Noted for its mainly AEC fleet, Machin's specialised in produce and general haulage. Two standard ISO containers would fit on a 40-foot trailer, which became possible after 1968. AEC's were purchased until the end of production and this well-known company ceased trading in 1991. (Negative A45731)*

Owen Aisher was a Kent builder who invented sand and cement roofing tiles because he tired of waiting for traditional clay tiles. His new tiles became hugely successful, leading to several Marley tile factories becoming established throughout the country. By 1971 a Mandator could carry sufficient tiles for an average sized family home plus all the necessary roofing felt and batons. *(Photo: Marley)*

The majority of Scottish long distance lorry drivers were true professionals and took great pride in their vehicles and also how they were sheeted and roped. With two main sheets and a flysheet this was as good as it gets. The Mandator was also quite smart, being operated in the Forth fleet that was part of the large Tayforth Group. *(Negative A35715)*

*Harp lager is of course brewed by Guinness, and was exported from their Dublin brewery in these tanks, shown in 1968 on a Mandator and drawbar trailer outfit. By then, trailers usually ran on twin wheels. Both lorry and trailer bodies had fixed back boards. Apparently there was a system of clamps for securing the containers. (Negative 41474)*

*Captured by the AEC Staff photographer on an almost deserted stretch of Motorway, Ross Poultry's Mandator and drawbar trailer was apparently going well. The Buxted brand of chicken, usually frozen, caused roast chicken to become a far more common meal, rather than a hitherto upmarket luxury. (Negative A50408)*

*The old model and its replacement side by side outside Daniel Stewart's depot at Blairgowrie in 1965. Both Tilt-cabbed and Mk.V Mandators were produced concurrently for a few months from about mid-1965 until spring 1966. Stewart's fleet is remembered for its rich, traditional Scottish livery and both AECs were on continental work. This company became part of Christian Salvesen, with its founder becoming Operations Director of the purchaser. (Negative C35482)*

*An early tilt-cabbed Mandator outside of the rolling mill at Port Talbot Steelworks. Operated by Blue Line Transport the lorry's load comprised two steel coils on its new maximum length 33-foot trailer. This was a tandem axle trailer with its rear bogie at the extremity, so with careful positioning of the coils it would have been possible to run the outfit at 32 tons gross weight without individual axle overloads. The majority of these early TG Mandators were rated for 30 tons gross. (Negative C34434)*

*The passage of time has not been kind to this transparency, but it is included for the sheer interest it provides. On a snowy day in the late 1960s Hawker Siddeley Aviation's Mandator was engaged on moving the fuselage of a Nimrod aircraft. Not a great deal of weight but an enormously valuable cargo. The Morris crew bus, along with the official police presence of the rare Austin 2200 patrol car, provided private escort –supposedly a recent innovation. More modern aircraft are only just replacing Nimrods.*
*(Negative LC5332)*

*Mandators in New Zealand had to work hard and often had to pull two trailers. Mid-Northland's 1972 (Leyland) AEC had Truscott tanks and was fitted with the optional 9-speed Fuller range-change gearbox. It was still in service in the early 1980s. (Photo: Rufus Carr)*

*Many modifications were carried out on Australian and New Zealand AECs. This Mandator had an Eaton-Hendrickson double drive bogie substituted for its single back axle and it also received a 13-speed Fuller gearbox. In service with Northern Co-operative Carrying Association it was at its home depot in Kaitaia, N.Z. in 1974. (Photo: Rufus Carr)*

*Spiers of Melksham did not withdraw its last Mandators from service until 1991, when its newest was fourteen years old and obsolete. In the 1980s this predominantly AEC fleet gained cult status and all of them had been bought by the Wiltshire firm second hand. Photographed crossing Tower Bridge in March 1976 with a load of Geest banana containers, this Mandator was then a recent acquisition. (Photo: Peter J. Davies)*

As Leyland began increasing its influence on AEC's affairs some export markets, and especially that of New Zealand received 'Leyland' Mandators. Gaynor Fussell's Mandator was photographed at Port Whangarei in 1972. (Photo: Rufus Carr)

Most of the major British oil companies used Mandators for distributing petroleum products and Texaco had one of the larger AEC fleets in the mid-1970s. This 1973 registered 2TG series Mandator was about to enter service with a brand new trailer. (Photo: M.V.M. Photography / Texaco)

*Still going strong at almost ten years old in 1975, Radiata Transport's Mandator with its usual two trailers used for carrying wood chips. This AEC's standard 6-speed gearbox was replaced with a 13-speed Fuller unit. Nelson is on the South Island of New Zealand. (Photo: Rufus Carr)*

*For a short period in the early 1970s there was a slight revival of sales of heavyweight rigid four wheelers for drawbar trailer work. Such outfits provided versatility and the maximum gross weight was identical to that of an artic. By then a second man in the cab was also unnecessary. This was an exceptionally smart Mandator and trailer with Tautliner bodywork, which was a relatively recent innovation in 1973. (Negative C49616)*

*This is how many Mandators saw out their days, as local shunting units. In this role they were popular with drivers because of their low cab entry height, and this made a shunter's job easier when he had to climb into a cab numerous times daily. This enabled several Mandators to survive and then be restored for restoration. (Photo: Author's collection)*

*One of two Mandators based at Jersey Airport for aircraft re-fuelling duties. With a full load of Jet A-1 fuel the gross weight was 19 tons, hence they were restricted to airport duties fully laden. The photo was taken in August 1989 when the Mandator was twelve years old. (Photo: Author)*

*Rather perversely as Mandator production was being phased out from 1976, several orders were received for long wheelbase rigids, mainly for drawbar trailer work. Heatons of St.Helens bought some, mainly for its contract with Fibreglass. This Mandator carried the firm's own livery. Note the massive fuel tank and the final, basic style of front grille fitted from early 1976. By then all the chrome trimming had been discontinued from tilt cabs. (Photo: Author's collection)*

*Looking a little worse for wear in March 1990, Jack Poulton's Mandator livestock float was fourteen years old and still used most days. It was new to an agricultural machinery dealer and has survived to the present day in preservation. (Photo: Author)*

# SECTION 5

# AEC Mammoth Minor 1965–1971

Undoubtedly, the 1964 Construction and Use Regulations brought Great Britain more into line with European countries in relation to maximum gross weights for lorries. However, British overall length limits still remained restrictive and axle spacing relative to imposed maximum legal loadings was problematic for achieving the full potential of 32 tons on four axles with articulated lorries. As explained in Section 4, it was quite straightforward to operate at 30 tons gross weight with a 33-foot tandem axle trailer and two-axle tractive unit. Many operators were at first content to settle for a payload of 20 to 20½ tons, as it was some 4 tons better than before. After carefully studying regulations, vehicle designers and customers soon realised that the extra weight could be obtained by various permutations of five axles articulated outfits. The cheapest means was with a tri-axle semi-trailer running on single wheels. Coupled to a Mandator, for example, this gave a payload of almost 22 tons, but because the trailer was still no longer than 33 feet, there was a risk of overloading the tractor's drive axle. Another option was a double drive 6x4 tractive unit, such as a Mammoth Major, but this was heavy and expensive for very little payload gain. Moreover, British hauliers had traditionally shunned 6x4 tractors except for heavy haulage work.

The best compromise for 32 tons was obtained with a twin steer, Chinese Six, tractive unit, or even a rear steer version. The latter describes a vehicle whereby a second steering axle is located immediately ahead of the driving axle. AEC's engineers opted for the former configuration and in 1965 their specially designed Mammoth Minor, 6x2 tractive unit was announced for operating at 32 tons gross train weight. The design weight was 36 tons if a heavy-duty back axle was fitted. Another advantage with such an axles layout was that weight tolerance was in-built by rating the tractor for 18 tons gross weight. By virtue of the chassis also having a longer wheelbase (12 feet 2½ inches) than a Mandator, the fifth wheel could be positioned to place some of the weight imposed by the laden trailer's kingpin onto the front axles. It provided an ideal solution; a relatively light tractor with good weight distribution and improved vehicle stability. There were also some innovative design features incorporated into Mammoth Minors to utilise limited chassis side rail space for essential items such as fuel tanks. Twin tanks of 48 gallons capacity were provided, with one hung on each side of the chassis frame, and to accommodate them air reservoirs were mounted transversely across the chassis behind the cab.

AEC had used the Mammoth Minor name for a lightweight rigid six-wheeler in the late 1930s, and for further details of this model and other AEC Chinese Sixes refer to *The AEC Mustang & Marshal*. The new, 1965, version was given chassis designation TG6RF and was based on the Ergomatic cabbed Mandator. Instead of the Mandator's single front axle of 5 tons, two lightweight axles were fitted under the Mammoth Minor. Each had a rating of 4 tons; therefore the combined weight limit was 8 tons. The lorry's driveline was identical to that of a Mandator with the same engine options from 1966. By having an extra axle with 6 inches wide brake shoes, the total braking area of a Mammoth Minor was 1,068 square inches. Hydraulic power assisted cam and double roller steering was supplied as an optional extra at first, but soon became standard. A stronger chassis frame than that of a Mandator was used for a Mammoth Minor, making it approximately ¾ of a ton heavier at 6 tons. The dimensions were 12 inches deep by 3 inches flange width. With a 33-foot flat trailer a potential payload of 21¼ tons was feasible.

However, the vast majority of Mammoth Minors entered service with tanker trailers. There were a couple of reasons for this. Firstly it enabled these specialised operators to maximise payloads with trailers that by nature of their construction were quite heavy unladen. Secondly, bulk liquids carriers believed a twin steering, 6x2 tractive unit gave better stability than a 4x2 design. As a consequence well-known tanker operators such as Air Products, James Hemphill Ltd., I.C.I., Tyburn Road Tankers Ltd., Stevenson Hardy Ltd., Alfred Manchester & Sons Ltd., and Conoco Petroleum (Jet), purchased scores of AEC Mammoth Minors.

Throughout the relatively short production run of Mammoth Minors any specification changes and options were identical to those applied to contemporary Mandators. In due course the AV760 engine became the only choice, a load-sensing valve was fitted into the braking system, and either a 10-speed manual splitter gearbox, or a 10-speed Pneumo-Cyclic semi-automatic transmission could be supplied.

In the year 1968 an amendment to the Construction and Use Regulations permitted 40-foot tandem axle trailers to be used in this country. This was to bring the United Kingdom into line with the rest of Europe, and also followed the introduction of ISO containers for exported and imported goods. The container ship revolution was in full swing for international trade leading to a long overdue modernisation of ports and working procedures in docks. ISO containers were standardised worldwide at either 20 or 40 feet long, so 40-foot trailers were needed to carry the longest containers. With 40-foot tandem axle trailers, 32 tons gross weight on four axles for articulated lorries was easy to achieve because individual axle overloading was not at risk if the outfit was loaded sensibly and correctly. Eventually, most transport firms would run four axle artics at 32 tons gross train weight irrespective of what commodities were being carried.

After the 1968 implementation of legislation allowing longer trailers it could be assumed that demand for AEC Mammoth Minors would have dwindled. This was not the case because they were popular tractive units and their inherent stability was still considered important. It was not until late in 1971 that the last were built. One of the reasons for this policy by operators, and chemicals and gasses hauliers in particular, was the fact that many of their trailers had been built for Mammoth Minors and were incompatible with two axle prime movers. As a general guide, a tanker trailer has twice the service life of a tractive unit, and for example, some built by such as Air Products for transporting pressurised and liquefied gasses were expensive to fabricate and manufacture. They were highly specialised, being designed to exacting specifications. Trailer kingpin positions were for Mammoth Minors and could not be easily altered to suit Mandators. Air Products persuaded AEC to build a final batch of six Mammoth Minors in mid and late 1971, after the model had been officially discontinued by Leyland, so that it could replace some of its earlier Chinese-Six tractors and so continue using its dedicated trailers, which were only halfway through their planned service life of 12-14 years.

During the six years in which AEC Mammoth Minors were available, approximately 2,200 were produced at Southall and probably all of them entered service with British companies. It is fairly certain that Air Products placed into service the last Mammoth Minors built, but these did not carry the highest chassis numbers recorded. AEC allocated chassis numbers against orders received even if a customer was scheduled to call off its chassis considerably later. The final two Air Products Mammoth Minors entered service on 1st December 1971. They were chassis numbers TG6RF 1725 and TG6RF 1814, with registration numbers KYF 579K and KYF 581K respectively. The highest Mammoth Minor chassis number recorded in Air Products fleet list is TG6RF 1974, KMX 497K, which entered service on 1st August 1971.

*This was either the second or third Mammoth Minor built and it can be seen what a well thought out chassis design it was. Air tanks were mounted transversely behind the cab to allow fuel tanks to be placed on each chassis rail, and the trailer air and electrical susies were easily accessible for the driver when he coupled to his trailer. (Negative A34153)*

*The role in which many Mammoth Minors were used, that is with tanker semi-trailers to maximise payloads at 32 tons gross weight. Improved stability was also claimed with a twin-steer layout. The AEC was a Tyburn Road Tank Services lorry on contract to British Hydrocarbon Chemicals Co. (Negative A37499)*

*Although the artic was covered in road grime its driver had found time to clean his Mammoth Minor's cab windows, a frequent necessity with tilt-cabbed AECs in wet conditions. Tyburn Road Tank Services had its head office at Wooburn Green, Bucks. and operated tankers nationally on both spot hire and contract work. (Photo: Author's collection)*

*By early 1967 Sam Anderson of Wilson Road, Newhouse, near Motherwell had almost 100 AECs of various types in his fleet, with half of them being Mandators. Some Mammoth Minors were purchased in 1966 for maximum weight operations. Steel bars from Hallside Steel Works at Cambuslang mostly comprised Anderson's traffic and with traditional high class Scottish livery this was a memorable AEC fleet. (Negative A38985)*

*Wet and dirty returning to Hemphill's depot off Rosyth Road, Polmadie, Glasgow, probably to purge its tank and wash down. This shot illustrates well how with this axles layout and combination it was possible to maximise the advantages of both maximum length and weight. (Negative 38967)*

*AEC did have a significant presence in many transport fleets that had "blue-chip" status. Long established Thomas Allen was one such customer. Quite often tanker trailers destined for European destinations were subjected to unaccompanied ferry crossings, with either associate companies, or contracted hauliers collecting trailers at the ferry terminal and delivering the contents.*
*(Photo: Author's collection)*

With the change to containerisation revolutionising docks' working practices in the late 1960s, 40-foot trailers able to hold either one, or two ISO containers were legalised in 1968. It also made for easier axle loading tolerances at 32 tons on four axles. However, such had been the scale of investment earlier in 33-foot trailers that demand for three axle tractive units continued. This smart Ferrymasters Mammoth Minor was registered in 1969 and was running on tubeless tyres. (Negative A45719)

A fine sideways profile of Fisons' Mammoth Minor exiting a roundabout. Note the absence of any other traffic; those were the days in late 1968. This was probably a slightly shorter tank trailer than the maximum allowed, judging by its position on the fifth wheel, and distance between tank and cab. (Negative 41944)

*Chancelot Mill of Leith, a subsidiary of Allied Mills in the mid-'60s, used Mammoth Minors for supplying bread flour to the Sunblest bakery at Gateshead. Note how the outfit was designed for maximum 32 tons weight; the trailer rear bogie was at the extremity, whilst the location of the fifth wheel on the tractor resulted in weight being imposed on all its axles for a well-balanced and stable outfit.*
*(Negative C43970)*

*By 1966 AEC was supplying all the heavy vehicle requirements of Air Products, including four Mammoth Minors in that year. Liquefied and pressurised gas tanker trailers were built in-house at the company's Acrefair factory. Some were designed to be compatible only with twin-steer tractive units, causing Air Products to request AEC to build a further batch of Mammoth Minors when the model had all but been discontinued in 1971-2. (Negative C36321)*

# SECTION 6

## Mandators And Mammoth Minors In Retrospect

Of all the important British commercial vehicles builders AEC was perhaps at its best in designing specific lorries for specialised duties. These were not radically different from other mainstream AECs and used concurrent engines, gearboxes, and axles. Yet engineers at Southall willingly accepted suggestions from operators and incorporated modifications and improvements into designs. Customer input frequently resulted in lorries for particular tasks that were superior to those of competitors. In the mid-1930s a market emerged for tough four wheelers capable of pulling drawbar trailers and AEC Matador Mk.IIs were manufactured in response. During the Second World War and the relaxation of overall vehicle length limits, drawbar trailers became more numerous behind eight-wheelers, so Matadors, (then they became Mandators), developed as fifth wheel tractive units. As drawbar prime movers, Matadors and Mandators were never as common as Leyland Beavers, despite being of lighter construction and capable of better payloads. This was mainly because AEC did not have the manufacturing capacity of its great rival. Until about 1960, lorry production was secondary to that of passenger vehicles.

From the mid-1950s onwards, and availability of "Tin-Front" Mk.IIIs, Mandators gained popularity as tractive units when the move to articulation began to gather momentum. At first this was a cautious change in policy by operators. Then by 1960 and Mk.V models, the pace quickened, and after 1965 when Ergomatic cabbed Mandators appeared there was a veritable rush to embrace the newest fashion in road transport. For about twelve years until approximately 1972 there was a halcyon period for AEC when Mandators were market leaders and other models were also popular. Lack of development, financial problems within British Leyland, and Scandinavian tractive units with superior specifications and more driver appeal ultimately dislodged the Mandator from its envied position.

In the years when Matador Mk.IIs, Mk.IIIs, and Mandator Mk.IIIs were travelling roads in Great Britain and overseas, these lorries were noted for their reliability and longevity. With 7.7 litre engines, then 9.6 or 11.3 litre units AEC was producing power units that were respected worldwide. AEC lorries were well designed and chassis were built to high engineering standards. After "Tin-Front" Mandators were introduced in the mid-1950s the mechanical specification was the best available from any British manufacturer. If extras such as overdrive gearbox and power assisted steering were specified, then for its time a Mandator Mk.III was quite an advanced lorry. The only criticism was of cabs, which were draughty, noisy and rather uncomfortable, no matter what coachbuilder assembled them.

When Mandator Mk.Vs appeared they were to a new design and coincided with the first phase of Britain's road transport revolution of the 1960s. Their impact was immediate and visually Mk.V cabs were extremely attractive, with styling that still appears modern over forty years later. From a driver's perspective the interior still had shortcomings with complaints levelled at Mk.III structures remaining valid. Early AV590 and AV690 engines gained some notoriety for frequent cylinder head gasket failures and leaking injector pipes. New gasket materials and improved, deeper, cylinder head nuts cured the former fault and modifications solved the latter problem. Improved 2AV590 and 2AV690 units with counter-balanced and dampened crankshafts were fine engines, with larger variants also capable of turbo-charging for high power, specialist installations.

Maybe all Mk.V tractive units would have benefited from having longer wheelbases, as front axle vibration was common with G4RA models. To remedy this fault it was recommended that shock absorbers were fitted retrospectively and that the fifth wheel coupling was re-sited further forward. Mandator 2G4RA tractive units did have hydraulic shock absorbers fitted during assembly. Arguably, '2 series' Mandator Mk.Vs were the first modern British designed tractive units. They had ample power to provide high cruising speeds and potential for fast journey times with excellent brakes. An engine output of 192 bhp was plenty of power in 1963 for 24 tons gross weight, and it is no surprise that these AECs became very popular with both drivers and company owners alike.

Ergomatic cabbed Mandators were able to capitalise on their predecessors' success when introduced in 1965. The new cab addressed all drivers' complaints with its soundproofing insulation, comfort, ease of entry, and magnificent vision. Tilt-cabbed Mandators had at least the power of Mk.Vs even though gross weights were increased. However AV691 engines in Ergomatic cabbed lorries were not entirely successful. They had rather thick cylinder liners in a dry liner design, which led to heat retention when the engine was working hard. Whilst the cab was an excellent working environment for the driver, it was used on a multitude of chassis made by AEC, Leyland, and Albion. Consequently, fitting a bulky engine such as an AV691 under the cab was not easy, and it restricted not only the radiator capacity, but also cooling airflow around the engine. Also, AEC was experimenting with novel coolant systems which were not fully proven. AV691 engines tended to overheat badly in demanding operating environments and pistons could pick up liners in consequence. Although the more powerful AV760 engine occupied identical space as an AV691, it had thinner liners and was far less susceptible to overheating. By 1968 AV691 engines had been discontinued for most lorry applications. Thereafter, AV760 engines were highly regarded for reliability and longevity, but Ergomatic cabbed AEC Mandators and Mammoth Majors still retained their reputations for overheating in hot climates overseas. Siting radiator header tanks behind cabs on 2TG4 versions, which also increased coolant capacity, did help to a greater extent.

AEC experienced problems with engine temperatures over the years, and another common fault in the early days of tilt-cabbed Mandators was also cooling related. In an attempt to save a little weight, AV691 and AV760 engines had 12-blade plastic fans mounted on the crankshaft pulley. Because of cab restraints outlined in the previous paragraph fans ran very close to radiators, and a peculiarity of plastic blades was their tendency to spread the faster they rotated. Consequently blades could catch the radiator causing them to detach and puncture the radiator core. Reverting to traditional metal fan blades prevented most such incidents in future.

When Leyland introduced Butec electrical components into AEC tilt-cabbed lorries initially there were some problems. Alternators were incapable of sustained high outputs and required modification. The patent holder, Leece-Neville of Ohio designed starter motors for totally enclosed flywheels as used in U.S.A., but British engines had open flywheels. This design caused starter motors to retain water thrown up by tyres and it was not unknown for AECs to mysteriously start up by themselves when unattended because starter motors shorted. Once again, design rectification was necessary.

Despite problems in the first months of tilt-cabbed Mandator production sales rocketed and once teething troubles had been resolved the model became reliable and productive. For years a Mandator was one of the most profitable maximum weight lorries to operate. Many a transport manager running an own account fleet of Mandators kept his financial director happy with low transport and distribution costs. Many a hire and reward haulier saw business prosper because of AEC Mandators. They were always very popular with Scottish operators, who were, and still are, some of the most discerning and critical people in road transport.

In the couple of years before the model was discontinued Mandators were becoming somewhat basic and out-moded. Road transport had advanced dramatically. Sometimes reliability was again suspect as the odd rogue lorry slipped through the inspection department. This was a direct consequence of under investment at Southall because of the precarious financial predicament of British Leyland. Manufacturing machinery needed repairing or replacement and some components failed prematurely because of faulty machine shop equipment. Nevertheless, some measure of the high regard AV760 engines won can be gauged from a table of results published in 1979 in "Transport Engineer", the journal of The I.R.T.E. This analysis reported a survey of 9,488 heavy lorry engines comprising 16 different makes. Details were for repair costs per 100,000 miles, excluding routine servicing and maintenance. AEC's AV760 came fourth at 0.452 pence per mile. Above were Cummins 250 (0.394 pence per mile), Gardner 8LXB (0.334 pence per mile) and Gardner 6LXB (0.265 pence per mile). It is sobering to note that one of the Leyland engines that Mandator customers persuaded to buy Leyland Buffalos would have endured showed costs of 1.591 pence per mile.

During the years of AEC Matador and Mandator production AEC engines were supplied to various competing chassis assemblers. Maudslay, a sister company within the ACV Group fitted 7.7 litre and 9.6 litre power units. Atkinson and ERF were supplied with 7.7 litre engines during World War Two, and throughout the 1950s Atkinson fitted 9.6 and 11.3 litre power units at the request of certain customers such as Whitbread and Harold Wood. Seddon of Oldham also used AV590, AV690 and 2AV690, AV691, and AV760 units in its heavyweight tractive units and multi-axle lorries. Overseas, Vanajan of Finland, Willeme of France, Berreiros of Spain, and O.M.T. of Italy all built lorries with these larger AEC engines of the 1950s and '60s. Industrial versions were used in numerous applications including cranes and excavators, construction industry plant and equipment, air compressors, pumping sets, and generators,

It is hard to recall a major British lorry operator without AEC Mandators at some period in its history. By 1964 BRS had over 500 Mandators in service, a mixture of Mk.IIIs and Mk.Vs. This organisation bought at least as many tilt-cabbed models in the next few years. Incidentally, BRS was one of very few customers allowed to call off lorries from the Southall production line without ordering in advance. The legendary Harold Wood was another accorded this privilege and his first Mandators were Mk.Vs in 1962. But consider this list of only a few Mandator operators. It includes some of the crème de la crème of British companies; Turners (Soham) Ltd., Hipwood & Grundy Ltd., Air Products, Shell-Mex & B.P. Shell, Esso, Mobil, Fina, Texaco, Jet Petroleum, Total Oil, Spillers Milling, RHM Agriculture, Sam Anderson, Munro of Aberdeen, Spiers of Melksham, John Jempson of Rye, Willmotts of Wells, R. Sinclair Transport, Tunnel Cement, Western Transport, Russell of Bathgate, I.C.I., Caledonian, Forth Road Services, Federated Transport, Pointers of Norwich. Several of these also ran Mammoth Minors.

When Leyland discontinued Mandator production in 1977 it can be understood why such a decision was taken in spite of unprecedented success enjoyed by the lorry in the preceding twenty years. Group model rationalisation was long overdue and the Mandator itself was in need of replacement by a new design that was more suitable for the demands of the late 1970s. Leyland L12 Buffalos offered little or none advancement over Mandators, save for an updated AEC engine. Leyland Marathons were adequate and had Southall ancestry, but were not every AEC purchaser's preference or choice. Many long-standing customers ultimately defected to Scandinavian and European makes.

AEC Mandators carved out a large and loyal following amongst drivers and operators. Even today, over 25 years after the last were made, rarely do former drivers or owners make criticism of them. They were highly regarded as fine lorries to drive, and renowned for excellent reliability, productivity, profitability, and mechanical longevity. Whether used as fleet tractive units by national companies, or as flagship lorries by small family firms they performed in both roles admirably and must be categorised as some of the best lorries of their time.

Quite simply AEC Mandators were classic British lorries of the twentieth century.

# APPENDIX A

## Chassis Designations And Details

### MATADOR 4x2

| DESIGNATION | ENGINE | IN PRODUCTION | NOTES |
|---|---|---|---|
| 346 | A162 (Petrol) | 1935-40 | Forward Control Mk.II |
| O346 | A171 (Oil) | 1935-40 | Forward Control Mk.II |
| 246 | A162 (Petrol) | 1935-40 | Normal Control Mk.II |
| O246 | A171 (Oil) | 1935-40 | Normal Control Mk.II |
| O347 | A173/A206 | 1946-48 | Forward Control Mk.II Interim |
| 3471 | A216 | 1948-50 | Forward Control Mk.III |
| 3472 | A221 | 1950-55 | Forward Control Mk.III Export Only |
| 3481 | A221 | 1955-57 | "Tin Front" Mk.III Export Only |
| 2481 | A216 | 1947-48 | Normal Control Mk.III Export |
| 2482/3 | A216/A221 | 1948-57 | Normal Control Mk.III Export |

### MATADOR 4x2 WHEELBASES

| MODEL | WHEELBASE | APPLICATION | GVW (SOLO) | GTW | NOTES |
|---|---|---|---|---|---|
| 346, O346 246, O246 O347, 3471 3472 | 12 Ft. 1 Ins. | Tipper | 12 Tons | 22 Tons | 246, O246, 3472 Fifth Wheel Tractive Unit For Export Only |
| 346, O346 246, O246 O347, 3471 3472 | 14 Ft. 7 Ins. | Tipper, Tanker, Flat Platform | 12 Tons | 22 Tons | 3472 Export Model Only |
| 346, O346 246, O246 O347, 3471 3472 | 16 Ft. 7 Ins. | Flat Platform | 12 Tons | 22 Tons | 3472 Export Model Only |
| O347, 3471 | 9 Ft. 6 Ins. | Tractive Unit | | 22 Tons | Fifth Wheel Artic. All Markets |
| 2481, 2482/3 | 12 Ft. 1 Ins. | Tractive Unit | | 22 Tons | Export Model |
| 2481, 2482/3 | 14 Ft. 7 Ins. | Tipper, Tanker, Flat Platform | 12 Tons | 22 Tons | Export Model |
| 2481, 2482/3 | 16 Ft. 7 Ins. | Flat Platform | 12 Tons | 22 Tons | Export Model |
| 3481 | 9 Ft. 6 Ins. | Tractive Unit | | 24 Tons | Export Model |

# MANDATOR (& MAMMOTH MINOR)

| DESIGNATION | ENGINE | IN PRODUCTION | NOTES |
|---|---|---|---|
| 669 & 645 | A162 (Petrol) | 1931-35 | Forward Control |
| 672 & 646 | A 162 (Petrol) | 1931-32 & 1934-35 | Normal Control |
| 3472/4/5 | A216 | 1950-55 | Forward Control Mk.III |
| 2472 | A221 | 1957-61 | Normal Control Mk.III |
| 3481/2/3/4 | A221 | 1955-60 | "Tin Front" Mk.III |
| G4RA | AV590/AV690 | 1959-63 | Mk.V |
| G4RA | 2AV590/2AV690 | 1962-63 | Mk.V |
| 2G4RA | 2AV590/2AV690 | 1963-66 | '2 series' Mk.V |
| TG4R | AV691/AV760 | 1965-71 | Ergomatic Cab Range |
| 2TG4R | AV760 | 1971-77 | Ergomatic Cab |
| TG6RF | AV691/AV760 | 1966-71 | 6x2 Tractive Unit |

## MANDATOR WHEELBASES

| MODEL | WHEELBASE | APPLICATION | GVW (SOLO) | GTW | NOTES |
|---|---|---|---|---|---|
| 3472/4/5 | 9 Ft. 6 Ins. | Tractive Unit | | 22 Tons | |
| 3472/4/5 | 12 Ft. 1 Ins. | Tipper | 12 Tons | 22 Tons | |
| 3472/4/5 | 14 Ft. 7 Ins. | Tipper, Tanker, Flat Platform | 12 Tons | 22 Tons | |
| 3472/4/5 | 16 Ft. 7 Ins. | Flat Platform | 12 Tons | 22 Tons | |
| 3481/2/3/4 | 9 Ft. 6 Ins. | Tractive Unit | | 24 Tons | "Tin Front" |
| 3481/2/3/4, 2472 | 12 Ft. 1 Ins. | Tipper | 14 Tons | 24 Tons | 2472 Tractive Unit |
| 3481/2/3/4, 2472 | 14 Ft. 7 Ins. | Tipper, Tanker, Flat Platform | 14 Tons | 24 Tons | |
| 3481/2/3/4, 2472 | 16 Ft. 7 Ins. | Flat Platform | 14 Tons | 24 Tons | |
| G4RA, 2G4RA | 8 Ft. 0 Ins. Or 10 Ft. 1 Ins. | Tractive Unit | | 24 Tons | 2G4RA Could Be Uprated to 30 Tons |
| G4RA, 2G4RA | 12 Ft. 5 Ins. | Tipper, Tanker | 14 Tons | 24 Tons | |
| G4RA, 2G4RA | 15 Ft. 2 Ins. | Tanker, Flat Platform | 14 Tons | 24 Tons | |
| TG4R, 2TG4R | 9 Ft. 6 Ins. | Tractive Unit | | 32 Tons | Early TG4R Models 30 Tons |
| TG4R, 2TG4R | 12 Ft. 1 Ins. | Tipper, Tanker | 16 Tons | 32 Tons | Some Export Models 14 Tons |
| TG4R, 2TG4R | 15 Ft. 0 Ins. | Tipper, Tanker, Flat Platform | 16 Tons | 32 Tons | Some Export Models 14 Tons |
| TG4R, 2TG4R | 18 Ft. 0 Ins. | Flat Platform | 16 Tons | 32 Tons | Some Export Models 14 Tons |
| TG6RF | 12 Ft. 2½ Ins. | Tractive Unit | | 32 Tons | Mammoth Minor |

# APPENDIX B

## Matador (4x2), Mandator, & TG6RF Mammoth Minor Engines

Power outputs have been corrected to a common database of the British Standards AU:141 1967 rating. It provides meaningful comparisons between earlier and later engines. BS conditions were set at 60 degrees Fahrenheit and 29.92 inches of mercury atmospheric pressure. Brake horsepower quoted is nett power available at the flywheel after deductions for power absorbed by engine auxiliaries. For further comparison with modern metric bhp ratings increase these figures by 9%.

**Understanding AEC engine designations:** A = AEC power unit. V = Vertical Layout. (H = Horizontal Layout). U = Unified Threads. "590" = Approximate Capacity In Cubic Inches. "2" = Series Prefix For Significant Changes. (T = Turbo-charged. G = Industrial Engine). All engines listed in this table were 6-cylinder units.

| TYPE | LITRES | Cu. Ins. | BORE (Mm) | STROKE (Mm) | LINER TYPE | BHP @ RPM | TORQUE Lbs./Ft. @ RPM | YEARS | NOTES |
|---|---|---|---|---|---|---|---|---|---|
| A162 | 7.04 | 431 | 110 | 130 | Dry | 120 @ 2,400 | 328 @ 1,300 | 1936-40 | Petrol (Mk.II) |
| A171 | 7.581 | 463 | 105 | 146 | Dry | 115 @ 2,000 | 325 @ 1,200 | 1936-38 | Indirect Injection 7.7 Litre (Mk.II) |
| A173 | 7.581 | 463 | 105 | 146 | Dry | 95 @ 1,800 | 310 @ 1,100 | 1937-40 | Direct Injection 7.7 Litre (Mk.II) |
| A173 | 7.581 | 463 | 105 | 146 | Dry | 105 @ 1,800 | 335 @ 1,100 | 1946-47 | Re-tuned 7.7 Litre "Interim" Type |
| A206 | 9.636 | 590 | 120 | 142 | Dry | 120 @ 1,800 | 410 @ 1,000 | 1946-47 | 9.6 Litre "Interim" Type |
| A216 | 9.636 | 590 | 120 | 142 | Dry | 125 @ 1,800 | 430 @ 1,000 | 1947-55 | 9.6 Litre (Mk.III) |
| A221 | 11.310 | 690 | 130 | 142 | Dry | 150 @ 1,800 | 505 @ 1,100 | 1955-61 | 11.3 Litre ("Tin Front" Mk.III) |
| AV590 | 9.636 | 590 | 120 | 142 | Wet | 125 @ 1,800 | 430 @ 1,000 | 1959-62 | AV590 (Mk.V) |
| AV690 | 11.310 | 690 | 130 | 142 | Wet | 150 @ 1,800 | 505 @ 1,100 | 1959-62 | AV690 (Mk.V) |
| 2AV590 | 9.630 | 590 | 120 | 142 | Wet | 158 @ 2,000 | 480 @ 1,200 | 1962-65 | Modified AV590 (Mk.V) |
| 2AV690 | 11.310 | 690 | 130 | 142 | Wet | 192 @ 2,000 | 560 @ 1,200 | 1962-65 | Modified AV690 (Mk.V) |
| AV691 | 11.310 | 690 | 130 | 142 | Dry | 187-218 @ 2,200 | 544-573 @ 1,200 | 1965-68 | Last Mk.Vs & Ergomatic Range |
| AV760 | 12.473 | 761 | 136 | 142 | Dry | 206-226 @ 2,200* | 588-618 @ 1,500 | 1966-77 | Ergomatic Range |

**Note:** 1. * Lower bhp setting was at 2,000 rpm.

2. AEC fitted various Simms, CAV, or Bosch in-line fuel injection pumps and rotary CAV DPA injection pumps.

3. AV690 was up-rated to 165 bhp @ 2,000 rpm for certain overseas customers.